DATE DUE			

JIMI HENDRIX

JIMI HENDRIX

Sean Piccoli

CHELSEA HOUSE PUBLISHERS
Philadelphia

Chelsea House Publishers
Editorial Director   Richard Rennert
Art Director   Sara Davis
Picture Editors   Adrian Allen, Judy Hasday
Production Manager   Pamela Loos

Staff for JIMI HENDRIX
Senior Editors   Philip Koslow, John Ziff
Senior Designer   Cambraia Magalhaes
Picture Researcher   Pat Burns
Cover Illustrator   Daniel O'Leary

3 5 7 9 8 6 4 2

Library of Congress Cataloging-in-Publication Data
Piccoli, Sean.
Jimi Hendrix: Sean Piccoli.
   p. cm.—(Black Americans of Achievement)
   Includes bibliographical references and index.
ISBN 0-7910-2042-8
       0-7910-2284-6 (pbk.)
1. Hendrix, Jimi—Juvenile literature. 2. Rock musicians—United States-
Biography—Juvenile literature. 3. Afro-American musicians—Biography—
Juvenile literature. [1. Hendrix, Jimi. 2. Musicians. 3. Rock music. 4.
Afro-Americans—Biography.] I. Title.
ML3930.H45P52 1996
95-38704
787.87'166'092—dc20   CIP
[B]   ACMN

Frontispiece: Jimi Hendrix performs a typically intense guitar solo during a 1968 concert.

CONTENTS

— ❧ —

BLACK AMERICANS OF ACHIEVEMENT

HENRY AARON
baseball great

KAREEM ABDUL-JABBAR
basketball great

ALVIN AILEY
choreographer

MUHAMMAD ALI
heavyweight champion

RICHARD ALLEN
*religious leader and
social activist*

MAYA ANGELOU
author

LOUIS ARMSTRONG
musician

ARTHUR ASHE
tennis great

JOSEPHINE BAKER
entertainer

JAMES BALDWIN
author

BENJAMIN BANNEKER
scientist and mathematician

AMIRI BARAKA
poet and playwright

COUNT BASIE
bandleader and composer

ROMARE BEARDEN
artist

JAMES BECKWOURTH
frontiersman

MARY MCLEOD
BETHUNE
educator

JULIAN BOND
civil rights leader and politician

GWENDOLYN BROOKS
poet

JIM BROWN
football great

STOKELY CARMICHAEL
civil rights leader

GEORGE WASHINGTON
CARVER
botanist

RAY CHARLES
musician

CHARLES CHESNUTT
author

JOHN COLTRANE
musician

BILL COSBY
entertainer

PAUL CUFFE
merchant and abolitionist

COUNTEE CULLEN
poet

BENJAMIN DAVIS, SR.,
AND BENJAMIN DAVIS, JR.
military leaders

MILES DAVIS
musician

SAMMY DAVIS, JR.
entertainer

FATHER DIVINE
religious leader

FREDERICK DOUGLASS
abolitionist editor

CHARLES DREW
physician

W. E. B. DU BOIS
scholar and activist

PAUL LAURENCE DUNBAR
poet

KATHERINE DUNHAM
dancer and choreographer

DUKE ELLINGTON
bandleader and composer

RALPH ELLISON
author

JULIUS ERVING
basketball great

JAMES FARMER
civil rights leader

ELLA FITZGERALD
singer

MARCUS GARVEY
black nationalist leader

JOSH GIBSON
baseball great

DIZZY GILLESPIE
musician

WHOOPI GOLDBERG
entertainer

ALEX HALEY
author

PRINCE HALL
social reformer

MATTHEW HENSON
explorer

CHESTER HIMES
author

BILLIE HOLIDAY
singer

LENA HORNE
entertainer

LANGSTON HUGHES
poet

ZORA NEALE HURSTON
author

JESSE JACKSON
civil rights leader and politician

MICHAEL JACKSON
entertainer

JACK JOHNSON
heavyweight champion

JAMES WELDON JOHNSON
author

MAGIC JOHNSON
basketball great

SCOTT JOPLIN
composer

BARBARA JORDAN
politician

MICHAEL JORDAN
basketball great

CORETTA SCOTT KING
civil rights leader

MARTIN LUTHER KING, JR.
civil rights leader

LEWIS LATIMER
scientist

SPIKE LEE
filmmaker

CARL LEWIS
champion athlete

JOE LOUIS
heavyweight champion

RONALD MCNAIR
astronaut

MALCOLM X
militant black leader

THURGOOD MARSHALL
Supreme Court justice

TONI MORRISON
author

ELIJAH MUHAMMAD
religious leader

EDDIE MURPHY
entertainer

JESSE OWENS
champion athlete

SATCHEL PAIGE
baseball great

CHARLIE PARKER
musician

GORDON PARKS
photographer

ROSA PARKS
civil rights leader

SIDNEY POITIER
actor

ADAM CLAYTON POWELL, JR.
political leader

COLIN POWELL
military leader

LEONTYNE PRICE
opera singer

A. PHILIP RANDOLPH
labor leader

PAUL ROBESON
singer and actor

JACKIE ROBINSON
baseball great

DIANA ROSS
entertainer

BILL RUSSELL
basketball great

JOHN RUSSWURM
publisher

SOJOURNER TRUTH
antislavery activist

HARRIET TUBMAN
antislavery activist

NAT TURNER
slave revolt leader

DENMARK VESEY
slave revolt leader

ALICE WALKER
author

MADAM C. J. WALKER
entrepreneur

BOOKER T. WASHINGTON
educator

IDA WELLS BARNETT
civil rights leader

WALTER WHITE
civil rights leader

OPRAH WINFREY
entertainer

STEVIE WONDER
musician

RICHARD WRIGHT
author

ON
ACHIEVEMENT
❧

Coretta Scott King

B<small>EFORE YOU BEGIN</small> this book, I hope you will ask yourself what the word *excellence* means to you. I think that it's a question we should all ask, and keep asking as we grow older and change. Because the truest answer to it should never change. When you think of excellence, perhaps you think of success at work; or of becoming wealthy; or meeting the right person, getting married, and having a good family life.

Those important goals are worth striving for, but there is a better way to look at excellence. As Martin Luther King, Jr., said in one of his last sermons, "I want you to be first in love. I want you to be first in moral excellence. I want you to be first in generosity. If you want to be important, wonderful. If you want to be great, wonderful. But recognize that he who is greatest among you shall be your servant."

My husband, Martin Luther King, Jr., knew that the true meaning of achievement is service. When I met him, in 1952, he was already ordained as a Baptist preacher and was working toward a doctoral degree at Boston University. I was studying at the New England Conservatory and dreamed of accomplishments in music. We married a year later, and after I graduated the following year we moved to Montgomery, Alabama. We didn't know it then, but our notions of achievement were about to undergo a dramatic change.

You may have read or heard about what happened next. What began with the boycott of a local bus line grew into a national movement, and by the time he was assassinated in 1968 my husband had fashioned a black movement powerful enough to shatter forever the practice of racial segregation. What you may not have read about is where he got his method for resisting injustice without compromising his religious beliefs.

He adopted the strategy of nonviolence from a man of a different race, who lived in a different country, and even practiced a different religion. The man was Mahatma Gandhi, the great leader of India, who devoted his life to serving humanity in the spirit of love and nonviolence. It was in these principles that Martin discovered his method for social reform. More than anything else, those two principles were the key to his achievements.

This book is about black Americans who served society through the excellence of their achievements. It forms a part of the rich history of black men and women in America—a history of stunning accomplishments in every field of human endeavor, from literature and art to science, industry, education, diplomacy, athletics, jurisprudence, even polar exploration.

Not all of the people in this history had the same ideals, but I think you will find something that all of them had in common. Like Martin Luther King, Jr., they all decided to become "drum majors" and serve humanity. In that principle—whether it was expressed in books, inventions, or song—they found something outside themselves to use as a goal and a guide. Something that showed them a way to serve others, instead of only living for themselves.

Reading the stories of these courageous men and women not only helps us discover the principles that we will use to guide our own lives but also teaches us about our black heritage and about America itself. It is crucial for us to know the heroes and heroines of our history and to realize that the price we paid in our struggle for equality in America was dear. But we must also understand that we have gotten as far as we have partly because America's democratic system and ideals made it possible.

We are still struggling with racism and prejudice. But the great men and women in this series are a tribute to the spirit of our democratic ideals and the system in which they have flourished. And that makes their stories special and worth knowing. 🙌

1

"A NEW AMERICAN ANTHEM"

BY DAYBREAK ON Monday, August 18, 1969, Max Yasgur's dairy farm in Bethel, New York, looked like a giant hole in the earth. A vast multitude, 400,000 strong, had occupied the land for several days, and as the crowd slowly dispersed, it left behind a sea of mud and debris. The only island in that sea was an elevated stage, built for a history-making event, and on August 18 the view from that stage was unforgettable: the Yasgur farm—soaked by rain, trampled underfoot, and littered with enough trash to choke a small city—could have passed for a refugee camp.

Such was the scene awaiting guitarist Jimi Hendrix and his band as they prepared to close the Woodstock Music and Arts Festival. Touted by its promoters as "three days of peace and music," Woodstock had become a reality on Yasgur's farm throughout a seemingly timeless weekend, as thousands of young people swayed under open skies and heavy rains, reveling in the music and sustaining a mood of hope and renewal that would define their generation. Organizers had lined up 25 acts, ranging from the blues-rock singer Janis Joplin to the British quartet known as the Who. Hendrix, the hottest rock guitarist of his day and a marvel to his fellow musicians, had insisted on closing the show. By the 18th, it appeared that he had made an unfortunate choice.

Surrounded by band members, technicians, and spectators, Hendrix brings the historic 1969 Woodstock Festival to a stirring conclusion.

Beset by technical problems and rain delays, Woodstock was running half a day late; some 320,000 people had already streamed away from the outdoor amphitheater. After experiencing three days of peace, music, rain, love, sex, drugs, food shortages, suffocating crowds, and ankle-deep mud, these pilgrims were sated and spent. They were migrating out, reversing the human tide that had poured into upstate New York over the weekend, creating one of the automotive age's single largest traffic jams—a 17-mile parking lot along Route 17B. The pioneers of the Woodstock Generation had, as they liked to say, done their thing; now they were going home.

The 80,000 people remaining were enough to fill a stadium but not 600 acres of farmland. Stragglers wandered through the tattered landscape like survivors of a mud slide, looking around as if wondering what had happened to everybody else. Woodstock was becoming a unique memory—no future event would ever quite duplicate its mixture of music, magic, misery, spontaneity, and history.

But the legend was not yet complete, as those who had left before the finale would realize to their regret. Woodstock's last act, Jimi Hendrix, walked onto the stage under a streaky morning sky with his white Fender Stratocaster electric guitar slung over one shoulder (he was left-handed, a rarity among guitarists) and his unruly black hair bound in a red headband that accentuated the planes of his broad, expressive face.

Hendrix looked like a cosmic hitchhiker, a cowboy gypsy clad in boots, bell-bottom jeans, a silver-studded belt, and a white fringed tunic with laces running up the front. The scattered crowd mustered a powerful roar to greet him. Hendrix surveyed the diehards who had waited three days and smiled.

"I see that we meet again," he said warmly. "Hmmm . . ."

His new band, Gypsy Sons and Rainbows, followed him onto the stage and took their places between the steel sound towers. Bassist Billy Cox, an old army buddy from Hendrix's days at Fort Campbell, Kentucky, was the first player Hendrix had called when British-born Noel Redding quit the original group, the Jimi Hendrix Experience, in June. Rhythm guitarist Larry Lee was another old friend and one of the few guitarists ever to share a stage with Hendrix. Percussionist Juma Sultan had played alongside legendary jazz artist John Coltrane. The second percussionist, Jerry Velez, had recently returned from the Vietnam War and was slowly readjusting to civilian life. Drummer Mitch

Basking in the August sun, some of the 400,000 Woodstock faithful survey the peaceful landscape of upstate New York. The three-day Woodstock festival, featuring many of the greatest names in rock and roll, was a unique event in American culture, defining the hopes and dreams of a generation.

Mitchell, another Briton, was the only holdover besides Hendrix from the Jimi Hendrix Experience, a band that in its short life changed pop music forever, melding rock, blues, funk, soul, and pop balladry in ways never before heard but widely imitated ever since.

From its 1966 debut in London, England, the three-man Jimi Hendrix Experience had conquered the rock world and its rapidly expanding arena circuit in three short years, becoming one of the biggest draws and highest-paid acts of its day. (Even at Woodstock, Hendrix pocketed $32,000 for closing the festival, almost three times what any other act there took home.) But restlessness—a constant, compulsive searching that colored his music and his life—drove Hendrix to challenge himself and his

Janis Joplin was among the rock and roll legends who performed at Woodstock. By choosing to be the festival's final act, following such stars as Joplin and the Who, Hendrix was confirming his status as rock's most extraordinary talent.

playing by shedding old skin and trying new things. The Jimi Hendrix Experience had been a classic power trio—guitar, bass, and drums. Hendrix's new band was twice that size.

The new lineup might someday be a stronger, sharper unit than the Experience, Hendrix believed, and closer to the spirit he sought in his music as he tried to move away from the arena-rock, power-trio pigeonhole. But there were problems. Hendrix had not played anywhere since the Experience's last gig, a stadium show in Denver that June. He had assembled his new group only a few weeks before Woodstock; it did not even have a name until Hendrix came up with Gypsy Sons and Rainbows on the morning of the performance.

During the weeks leading up to Woodstock, the new band's talented players were not gelling as everybody had expected. Daily practice sessions only highlighted their lack of chemistry and cohesion. "I got the feeling several times during rehearsals," Mitch Mitchell wrote in his 1990 memoir, *Jimi Hendrix: Inside the Experience*, "that Jimi realized it wasn't working and just wanted to get the gig over and start again."

The band continued to rehearse for about three weeks at a country house near Woodstock. They would not know how good or bad they were until they faced a mass of rock and roll fans who had already spent the weekend feasting on some of the best pop music ever played.

Despite the goodwill that prevailed at Woodstock, the Hendrix band had its work cut out for it. The sound system, plagued all weekend by rain and electrical storms, threatened to blink out at any second. Thousands in the crowd were walking barefoot over buried power lines that had now been uncovered by rain, runoff, and pedestrian traffic. The stage had also sunk several inches into the soft ground, pitching forward like a ship in rough seas.

The damp, sultry climate was playing havoc with equipment, throwing weather-sensitive guitars and basses completely out of tune.

On top of the challenges posed by the prevailing conditions, Hendrix had another adversary to manage: himself. Despite the infusion of new blood into

Toward the end of his two-hour set at Woodstock, Hendrix launched into an anguished, impassioned version of "The Star-Spangled Banner" that electrified the audience, expressing all the fury and heartbreak of the American experience during the 1960s.

his lineup, Hendrix came to Woodstock distracted and drained from the tremendous demands of his performance schedule.

Backstage at Woodstock on Sunday night, with his managers and handlers still negotiating with the organizers, Hendrix fell ill, possibly from drinking tainted water, and staggered into a medical tent, where he collapsed onto a cot. He recovered later in the night.

He was still Jimi Hendrix, a guitar-burning font of energy, an electric shaman who played the blues as if he were possessed. But the "Voodoo Chile," as he proclaimed himself in one of his fiery songs, was aging. He had packed several lives into his 26 years, and the overload often showed in his face. Everything seemed to be happening to Hendrix at an accelerated pace.

For Hendrix at Woodstock, the future was now. It was a moment to plug into and play. The band, incorrectly introduced as the Jimi Hendrix Experience, took a moment to get acquainted with the roaring crowd. Hendrix gently corrected the announcer's lapse. "Dig," he started, "we'd like to get something straight: we got tired of Experience and every once in a while we was blowing our minds too much. So we decided to change the whole thing and call it Gypsy Sons and Rainbows. For short, it's nothing but a band of gypsies."

Hendrix talked to crowds the same way he played—in a cascade of words and phrases that danced rhythmically off his tongue. The last remark hinted at things to come: by the fall of 1969, Hendrix would drop his Woodstock ensemble and form a new trio called Band of Gypsys, with Cox on bass and Buddy Miles on drums. The experiment that Woodstock represented was brief, although in Hendrix's short life and career, the few months he devoted to it were considerable.

"Jimi, are you high?" somebody yelled. It sounded like an offer rather than an accusation.

"I have mine," Hendrix replied. "Thank you very much."

The six-piece group tore into the Experience hit "Fire," a double-speed version in which Hendrix seemed to pull his bandmates along by the fury of his playing. He followed with a new song, "Isabella," which he said was "dedicated to maybe a soldier in the Army singin' about his old lady that he dreams about, and hugging a machine gun instead. Or it could be a cat, maybe, trying to fall in love with that girl."

For his third song, "Hear My Train A-Comin'," Hendrix slowed the tempo to a bluesy shuffle. He wound the tune out, turning the number into a long, slow jam. For eight minutes, he silenced the crowd with a breathtaking show of free-form soloing, making up phrases and musical passages as he went along—his band was in tune and in step, despite its shaky legs. Note by note, Hendrix would push the song upward to a moment of excruciating tension, a breaking point, and punch through the invisible barrier with an explosive, arching wail coaxed from his guitar and then a rush of notes. It was vintage Hendrix: sounds pouring from his instrument like inner voices screaming for release.

The band's two-hour set ran through the guitarist's personal time line, alternating between straight recitals of past works and rambling, experimental essays that told of things yet to be. "He was looking for a way out of the black acid-stud/guitar hero cul de sac," *Rolling Stone* magazine's David Fricke wrote in the liner notes to *Woodstock: Three Days of Peace and Music,* a 25th-anniversary retrospective on compact disc. "And yet somehow, that morning, he found real moments of daylight."

Some moments were better than others. Instruments refused to stay in tune. Sometimes the band's rawness showed. "Yeah, I know," Hendrix told the audience at one point, "we're tuning up between every single song, and this is not together and that's not together. We ain't all in uniform!" He also broke a guitar string while playing "Voodoo Chile," a song he introduced to the crowd as "a new American anthem, until we get a better one."

Hendrix, as it turned out, had one more anthem to play. Toward the end of the set he stepped away from his microphone and, like a lonely bugler, sounded out the first notes of a song everybody in the audience knew by heart: "The Star-Spangled Banner." The familiar melody floated out over the Woodstock crowd, across a field that looked like a war zone, in a baleful tone that seemed to weep under layers of amplified distortion. The space between each note Hendrix played felt a mile wide.

Something unprecedented was happening: Hendrix was taking America's national anthem and turning it into a national dirge. The crowd listened raptly, many mouthing the words as he played. Hendrix followed the melody faithfully, then cut away from the verses at key moments, bringing the "rockets' red glare" and "bombs bursting in air" to life with his Stratocaster, which had suddenly turned into a war machine. The amplifiers unleashed the deafening roar of high explosives and the rattle of gunfire, all of it generated by a lone guitarist creating a nightmarish vision of a star-spangled flag fluttering over a nation embroiled at that very moment in a bloody, unpopular war in Vietnam. Hendrix's guitar seemed to mock and revere the national anthem's grandiosity all at once. His electrified cry of emotion echoed in the hearts and minds of the audience.

Hendrix did not actually end his set with "The Star-Spangled Banner," but the song became Woodstock's capstone, a defining moment that witnesses, listeners, other players, and music critics would revisit again and again. "At that moment, he became one of the greats, like [John] Coltrane or [Charlie] Parker or [Eric] Dolphy," rock guitarist Vernon Reid recalled in a 1989 reminiscence. "He plugged into something deep, something beyond good or bad playing. It was just 'there it is.'"

Woodstock propelled Hendrix into a burst of renewed activity. He spent the following year the way he had spent the previous three: touring and recording. He crisscrossed the United States and Europe, with few breaks. He went into studios to record whenever time allowed and filled hundreds of hours of reel-to-reel tapes with songs, song fragments, and extended jams. The material, much of it still unreleased years later, could fill several albums. There was an urgency to Hendrix's activity after Woodstock, as if he knew he were racing to find or finish something before time ran out.

"I'm not sure I will live to be twenty-eight years old," he told Denmark's *Morgenposten* newspaper in 1970. His prediction proved correct. ⬥

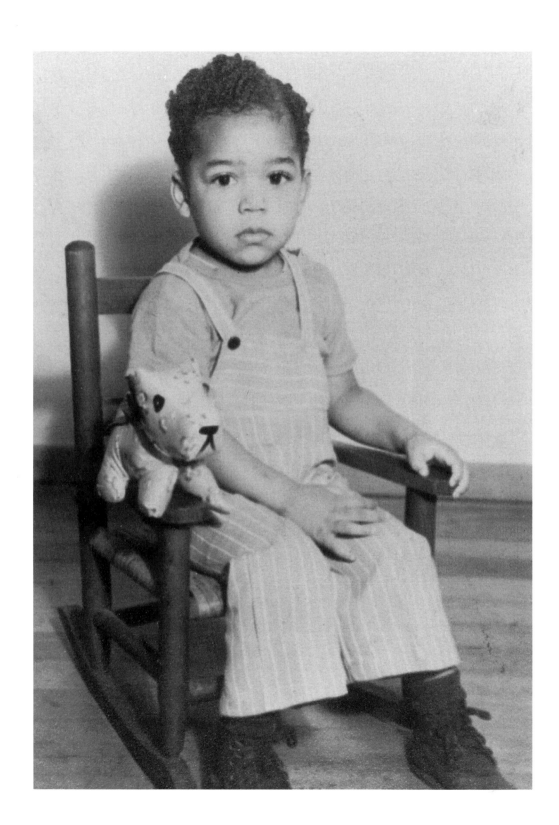

2

VOODOO CHILD

JOHNNY ALLEN HENDRIX was born on November 27, 1942, in Seattle, Washington, into a family with show business roots. His paternal grandparents, Nora and Ross Hendrix, once belonged to a vaudeville company, traveling performers who zigzagged across the country during the early 20th century, living out of suitcases and stopping wherever a paying audience could be found. Nora danced in the troupe's chorus line, and Ross was a stagehand. In 1911, the company hit Seattle and went broke. The road had carried the Hendrixes to the edge of America, the Pacific Northwest, and there it stopped. Stranded, they decided to give up their gypsy way of life. They boarded a ferry at Seattle's Victoria Station and crossed the gray waters of Puget Sound to Vancouver, Canada, where they settled down to live.

Nora and Ross Hendrix had four children between 1913 and 1919. The youngest, James Allen, or Al, was a small and wiry youngster who grew up hearing about his parents' vaudeville experiences and imagined himself getting up on the stage someday. Al inherited his mother's love of dancing; he developed into a talented, agile tap dancer who lit up nightclubs in the 1930s, first in Vancouver, then in Seattle, where he had moved to find work and make a life for himself.

Even during the Great Depression of the 1930s, Seattle was a place with possibilities. The rain-

Johnny Allen Hendrix at the age of three. The following year, when Al Hendrix returned from military service, he would rename his son James Marshall Hendrix.

shrouded city had graduated from logging, its original source of wealth, to steel, shipbuilding, and aircraft manufacturing. Seattle had enough people and commerce to support a healthy music scene, though the clubs and the musicians were segregated by race. It was here that Al Hendrix met Lucille Jeter, a pretty and delicate teenage girl with mocha-colored skin who loved the popular dances of the day—the Charleston, the jitterbug, the lindy hop—as much as Hendrix did. Hendrix and Jeter went dancing on their first night out and started dating regularly. Though Hendrix was struggling to find work, he and Jeter were young enough not to worry. They had few cares beyond where they might go jitterbugging on any given night.

The United States's entry into World War II changed everything. In December 1941, Japanese forces carried out a devastating surprise attack on the U.S. military base at Pearl Harbor in Hawaii. Early the following year, Hendrix was drafted into the army and knew that he would soon be shipping out. He and Lucille decided to marry. He was 22; she was 16 and pregnant. The young couple were wed on March 31, 1942, and soon after that the army sent Al Hendrix to Oklahoma for his basic training.

Johnny Allen Hendrix was born eight months later in Seattle's Kings County Hospital to a teenage mother who was too young, too poor, and too sick to care for her child alone. Al knew how much Lucille needed his help from the letters she wrote, and he desperately wanted to be back in Seattle. His superiors learned of the situation and, suspecting that he was planning to desert the army, threw him in the stockade "on general principles." (No charges were ever brought against him.) Hendrix was then transferred to several different bases around the country and finally sent halfway across the Pacific Ocean, to the Fiji Islands, to fight

Lucille Jeter Hendrix, Jimmy's mother, married at 16 and found it difficult to cope with the responsibilities of family life. She left home when Jimmy was seven and died eight years later.

the Japanese. He would not see his son until the war ended in 1945. By then young Johnny was three years old and living with friends of the Hendrixes in Berkeley, California. Al picked him up and brought him back to Seattle. He and Lucille were reunited, and a second son, Leon, was born in 1948.

The Hendrixes never had much money; they struggled just to survive. But the family was always rich in history and spirit. The Hendrix line had originated in the old American Indian country in Georgia and Tennessee, where Nora Hendrix's Cherokee ancestors had lived for centuries. The path that carried the Hendrixes to Seattle crossed the former slave states of the Deep South, where Lucille Jeter's parents grew up, and wound through African-American communities in Ohio and Chicago, where Ross Hendrix spent his youth. From

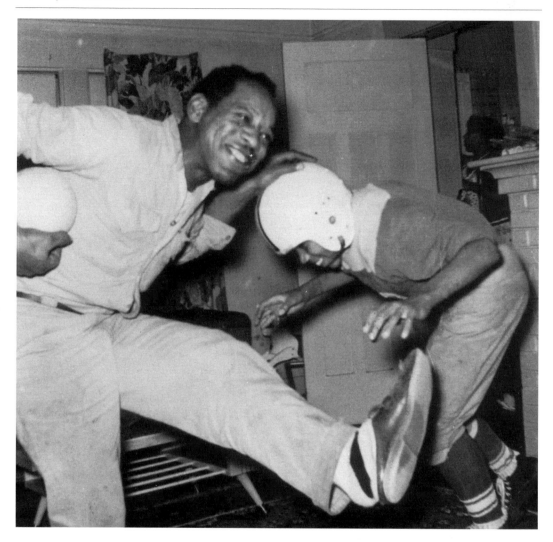

Though Al Hendrix often had to leave Jimmy in the care of friends and relatives while he struggled to earn a living, father and son were usually together on weekends, often playing football, as shown here. Not surprisingly, Jimmy became an avid football player when he grew older.

there, the trail stretched west and north to Washington State and Canada. Music, wanderlust, and a love of performance ran through the generations like rainwater drawn through the roots of a tree. The Hendrixes were a band of gypsies unto themselves, always in motion; young Johnny would grow up like his grandmother, Nora, a free spirit who called the road home.

Johnny would also grow up with a different name. In 1946, Al Hendrix changed his son's name from Johnny Allen to James Marshall, in honor of an older brother, Leon Marshall Hendrix, who had died when Al was a boy. Al Hendrix also did not want his son growing up with the same first name as John Williams, a Seattle man who had been seeing Lucille while Al was in the army. So Johnny was now Jimmy.

Even after the family was reunited, Jimmy's home life remained unstable. Al Hendrix struggled to make a steady living, and Lucille still found it difficult to accept the burdens of a family. She was often absent from home, and finally, in 1951, she and Al split up for good. Jimmy grew up amid a succession of relatives and family friends, moving through a series of houses, apartments, and rented rooms stretching from Vancouver to Texas. Somehow, he always found his way back to his father and baby brother in Seattle. He liked to visit his grandmother Nora in Canada—his grandfather Ross had died before Jimmy was born—and hear tales of her vaudeville days. "My grandmother used to tell me beautiful Indian stories," Hendrix said in a 1967 interview. "I used to see her a lot, you know, and she used to make these clothes for me. . . . I used to go back and take these clothes to school and wear them and all that, and you know, people would laugh."

During this time, Lucille Hendrix had three more children (a son and two daughters) by other men. When Jimmy was in Seattle, he and Leon would sometimes slip away, without their father's knowledge, to visit their mother across town. In 1958, Lucille Hendrix died of cirrhosis of the liver, caused by excessive drinking. She was 32 years old. Jimmy was 15.

The family's instability drew the scrutiny of social workers, who left Jimmy under his father's care but placed his younger brother, Leon, in a series of foster homes. Al often held down two jobs at a time and also studied radio repair in night school.

As a result, he could not spend much time at home. Instead, he would take Jimmy to the homes of various friends and relatives who would care for the boy until Al was free to take him back home. Sometimes father and son could only be together on the weekend. Not surprisingly, Jimmy retreated inward, finding comfort and stability in his private world. Shy and imaginative, he drew pictures and wrote stories, constructing a vivid universe of planets and stars. One of the few school subjects to hold his interest was art, which allowed him access to an infinite inner space where the troubles that pressed on his daily existence could not touch him. In this creative sphere, Jimmy's interest in music began to flourish.

One of the most cherished of Al Hendrix's scant possessions was a record collection featuring jazz artists Al had danced to with Lucille in happier days and blues records by early pioneers such as Muddy Waters and T-Bone Walker. Jimmy heard these records almost from infancy, and the blues recordings caught his attention most. "The first guitarist I was aware of was Muddy Waters," he later recalled. "I heard one of his old records when I was a little boy and it scared me to death."

The ghostly sound of Mississippi Delta blues also intrigued Jimmy, and he wanted to play what he heard. He got his first musical instrument, a harmonica, at age four, and this was followed by a one-string ukulele and an acoustic guitar. The guitar originally belonged to the son of the Hendrix's landlord. The boy told Jimmy he was willing to sell the guitar for five dollars, and Jimmy excitedly told his father about the offer. At that time five dollars was a fair amount of money to Al Hendrix; but he could see that the guitar was a quality instrument and that Jimmy really wanted it. "Sounds like a good deal to me," he said and gave Jimmy the money for his first real guitar.

Assuming his distinctive left-handed playing stance, a young Jimmy Hendrix poses for the camera in front of his house.

Although Jimmy was right-handed, he restrung the guitar backward so he could play it left-handed because it felt more natural when he used his right hand on the neck. "I didn't know a thing about tuning," he later recalled, "so I went down to the store and ran my fingers across the strings on a guitar they had there. After that I was able to tune my own."

He played day and night, absorbing everything he could from records, the radio, and other musicians he heard around the neighborhood and in clubs, which he had to sneak into because he was underage. He schooled himself on the blues artistry of B. B. King, Muddy Waters, John Lee Hooker, and Elmore James. Seattle radio, meanwhile, was crackling with a hot new sound that a New York deejay named Alan Freed had christened rock and roll. Jimmy hit his teens just as rock and roll was emerging from its country-and-blues cradle, and the new sound thrilled him. He loved the way the guitars drove Eddie Cochran's "Summertime Blues" and Chuck Berry's "Johnny B. Goode." He loved the frenzy Elvis Presley whipped up with his voice on "That's All Right Mama" and "Jailhouse Rock."

Jimmy would sit down in front of the record player with his guitar in his lap every day and force himself to play the same passages over and over, until every note, every phrase, felt and sounded right. "The way I felt about tap dancing is the way Jimmy felt about guitar playing," Al Hendrix later said. "I mean, it was just in him to do it. . . . I'd come home from work and he'd be there, plunk, plunk, plunk. . . . He'd be plunking away, and I could almost see his vision of himself playing for a band." From long hours of practice, Jimmy slowly began to create his own sound and style.

Later, Al brought Jimmy to Myers Music Store in Seattle and bought him a white Supro Ozark electric guitar, the first he ever owned. In the summer of 1959, Jimmy joined up with a group of neighborhood teenagers to form his first band, the Rocking Kings. He plugged his guitar into a borrowed amplifier and, with that setup, played bass for the six-piece band. In this modest, anonymous way, a one-man revolution in popular music began.

Al was concerned about his son's schoolwork but gave Jimmy permission to rehearse and play. The Rocking Kings performed at private parties, dance halls, picnics, and clubs throughout 1959 and 1960, playing the hits of the day: "Searchin'" and "Yakety Yak" by the Coasters; "At the Hop" by Danny Brown and the Juniors; "The Twist" by Hank Ballard; and "The Peter Gunn Theme" by Henry Mancini, whose locomotive bass-guitar riff Jimmy loved.

"I remember my first gig was at an armory, a National Guard place," Hendrix later recalled,

"and we earned 35 cents apiece." The Rocking Kings played in Seattle and Vancouver and landed a regular gig on teenage dance nights at a Seattle club called Birdland, where someone stole Jimmy's guitar. After summoning the courage to tell his father what had happened, Jimmy was able to replace the stolen Supro with a white Danelectro that he painted red. The Rocking Kings gradually built a following, and in 1960 they took second place in the All-State Band of the Year contest in Seattle. During that time, Jimmy was also gigging with a band called the Velvetones.

Jimmy was required to play bass parts on his guitar, but sometimes his bandmates allowed him to step forward and play a solo. Now and then he

In 1959, Jimmy joined a group of fellow teenagers to form the Rocking Kings. Though Jimmy's role was to play the bass part on his guitar, he was occasionally allowed to step up and play a solo.

would take solos without permission, discarding his bass part for an instant so he could juice up the song with an unexpected flourish of notes. Jimmy took all the enjoyment he could from these moments. He was delighted with the way the audience responded to his playing.

Jimmy's music was a great solace to him because the world beyond the bandstand could be cruel. Because of the tightness of the family budget his clothes were sometimes ragged, and there were boys at school who mocked and bullied him on this account. Once, when he went to church with worn-out shoes, the only ones he had, he was turned away at the door; the incident disturbed him deeply—he felt that God cared about what was in his heart, not about what was on his feet. But Jimmy endured the insults and the bullying; he had faith in himself and would not let a few bruises and bloody lips stop him from pursuing the dream that had completely taken hold of his heart. "It was his talent as a musician that gave Jimmy a measure of self-confidence rarely found in somebody with his kind of disrupted background," Harry Shapiro and Caesar Glebbeek wrote in *Electric Gypsy.*

Like most bands, the Rocking Kings eventually ran out of steam and changed directions. A few members quit. Jimmy stayed on but switched from bass to lead guitar. The new combo called itself Thomas and the Tomcats, after its leader, James Thomas, who had founded the Rocking Kings. Jimmy devoted a great deal of energy to the revamped band—when he was not in school or at home, he was playing and rehearsing nearly all the time. His father told him to keep at it and also urged him to raise his grades and graduate—he only had a few months to go at Seattle's Garfield High School. But Jimmy dropped out in October 1960. He felt that he had learned all he could at school, and he was ready for a taste of the real world.

For a while, Jimmy went to work in his father's gardening business, but he soon became restless. He wanted more out of life, and he knew the guitar was his ticket to something better. Unfortunately, his taste for adventure sometimes got him into trouble. One night he and a group of buddies broke into a department store and stole some clothes. They were caught, but the store decided not to press charges. Then, in May 1961, he was arrested while joyriding with friends in a stolen car. After a stint in a juvenile detention center, Jimmy went before a judge who gave him a two-year suspended sentence.

As an 18-year-old high school dropout with a criminal record, Jimmy had few prospects of making a living. There was a traditional alternative for young men in his position—the armed forces. Jimmy had already been classified as fit for service by his local draft board, and sooner or later he would be called up. He had no problem with this because he had always had strong patriotic feelings; he had even talked with his father about becoming a paratrooper and had gone to the local recruitment office to get information. If he waited to be drafted, however, he would be assigned to whichever unit the army picked for him. In order to be a paratrooper, he would have to enlist for a three-year hitch.

Jimmy went to the recruiting office in Seattle once more, this time to have his papers processed and his entry into the U.S. Army cleared. He was following in his father's footsteps, walking through the same door into the world outside, though he was doing it by choice. On May 31, 1961, he arrived at Fort Ord, California, for basic training, with a few dollars in his pocket. He was not allowed to bring his guitar. ꙮ

3

LITTLE WING

❦

"GO—GO—GO!" The jumpmaster slapped the young recruit on the backside and yelled into his ear. James Hendrix, serial number RA 19693532, hovered at the edge of the platform, 34 feet up, and saw the cable fastened to his body harness trailing away from the jump tower, toward the ground. He hesitated for a second. Then he was away, in gravity's tow, falling like a rock. "All of a sudden," Hendrix recalled in a letter to his father, "when all the slack was taken up on the line, I was snapped like a bullwhip and started bouncing down the cable." He hurtled toward the ground with his legs together and his chin against his chest and plowed into a sand dune—his first jump as a paratrooper-in-training. The landing was not graceful. But it was a start, and Hendrix was where he wanted to be.

Fort Campbell, Kentucky, served as the jump school for the 101st Airborne, known as the Screaming Eagles, an elite paratroop division with a distinguished combat record in World War II. Hendrix's dream was now to earn his Screaming Eagle, the distinctive sleeve patch worn by the men of the high-flying 101st.

He had spent the summer and fall in basic training at Fort Ord, hoping impatiently for word of his next assignment. Finally, the army had granted his request to go to jump school. Hendrix was thrilled. The notion of flight was intoxicating to a young man who daydreamed about the heavens and the

Hendrix in uniform in 1960, at Fort Ord, California. After finishing his basic training at Fort Ord, Hendrix realized his dream of becoming a paratrooper when he was assigned to the legendary 101st Airborne Division.

cosmos. He wanted to experience the sensation of an aircraft lifting him up. He wanted to breathe the air a mile above the earth and briefly exist in that endless blue space, with the ground spread out like a blanket waiting to catch him. He learned quickly at Fort Campbell and was jumping out of airplanes within weeks. At times he would board the craft with a camera and take pictures while falling. He included these aerial snapshots in his frequent letters home. "It's just as much fun as it looks," read the note on the back of one picture Al Hendrix received, "if you keep your eyes open (smile)."

In January 1962, eight months into his new career, Hendrix wrote home to ask for his red guitar, which his father wrapped and mailed from Seattle. Army life had not diminished Hendrix's love of music; if anything, the strict round-the-clock routines made him miss the freedom of playing more acutely than ever. Long before his own guitar arrived, Hendrix was borrowing instruments from fellow soldiers or checking them out of the recreation room in order to practice. And once the red Danelectro was back in his hands, he rarely let it out of his sight. He inscribed the name of a Seattle girlfriend, Betty Jean, on the guitar's body and played the instrument whenever he had a free moment. Some nights, he fell asleep in his bunk with the guitar still in his hands.

As he played, Hendrix sought to express through music the sounds and sensations of skydiving. He was also trying to master the eerie backcountry blues he heard in towns around Fort Campbell. One day, a fellow paratrooper named Billy Cox was walking past one of the base's service clubs when he heard an extraordinary sound—"somewhere between Beethoven and John Lee Hooker," as he would later put it—drifting out of the window. He went inside and found Hendrix playing guitar. The two soldiers started talking. Cox,

it turned out, came from a musical family. His mother was a pianist, and his uncle played saxophone with Duke Ellington. Cox himself played bass. He and Hendrix started jamming and quickly agreed to form a band. These were the first exchanges in a friendship that would last throughout Hendrix's life.

Cox and Hendrix found a drummer and a singer at Fort Campbell, and soon they were playing at the service clubs on the base and at bars in nearby towns. The group's first gig was at a place called the Pink Poodle Club in Clarksville, Tennessee.

Hendrix, Billy Cox, and Leonard Moses formed the King Kasuals at Fort Campbell, Kentucky, in 1962. After adding a drummer, vocalist, and saxophone player, the band played numerous dates both on and off the army base.

The band went through various lineups, with Cox and Hendrix always at the core, and eventually settled in as a quintet calling itself the King Kasuals. When not on duty the King Kasuals played off base, traveling as far away as the Carolinas. Usually they covered songs by popular artists, such as "Quarter to Three" by Gary "U.S." Bonds and "Tossin' and Turnin' " by Bobby Lewis. Hendrix also found that he had developed a small following among clubgoers and guitar players in the area around Fort Campbell.

These dates were not especially profitable, and Hendrix often complained in letters home about the meagerness of his army pay. Whenever possible, Al Hendrix wired his son a few extra dollars for spending money, a favor that Jimmy later returned when he began to earn good money as a musician. Some of Hendrix's biographers have stated that his imaginative nature made him a misfit in the army and that he was deeply disenchanted with life at Fort Campbell. However, family members have maintained that his letters always expressed his pride in being a Screaming Eagle and that he had no desire to leave the army. In any case, his military career came to a sudden end when he hurt his back during a parachute jump. The injury left him unfit for active duty, and he was given an honorable discharge.

Hendrix left Fort Campbell in the summer of 1962, slightly more than a year after joining the army. He phoned home and said that he would not be coming back to Seattle because he felt that there was nothing for him there. His father understood how he felt and encouraged him to go wherever he could find the most opportunity as a musician. Hendrix's first stop was nearby Clarksville; he waited there for Cox, who was discharged two months later. The two revived the King Kasuals and relocated to Nashville, Tennessee—Music City, U.S.A.

The home of country music's Grand Ole Opry, Nashville also had a bustling rhythm and blues scene. The Kasuals started playing Nashville clubs, but for very little money. Hendrix and Cox often depended on friends or nightclub managers for basics like food and shelter. Hendrix was good-looking, talented, and charming; there always seemed to be somebody willing to put him up or see that he did not starve on his meager musician's wages. One group of young Nashville women who were fond of Hendrix jokingly called themselves the Buttons because they sewed and mended his stage clothes. Meanwhile, Hendrix kept playing. He sat in girlfriends' apartments, plucking songs. In a town full of gifted musicians, where the level of skill was high and competition was fierce, Hendrix began to carve out a reputation as a serious player.

In Nashville, Hendrix also met and became friends with guitarist Larry Lee. Hendrix, Cox, and Lee would one day share the stage at Woodstock. But in Nashville they were just a gang of poor, hopeful musicians, hanging out and jamming together, sleeping under other people's roofs. What they lacked in money and steady work, they seemed to make up in confidence and daring: Hendrix and Lee would often go out and challenge other guitarists to jamming duels onstage. Nashville was Hendrix's early proving ground. "In the bars I used to play in," he later said, "we'd get up on the platform where the [electric] fan was. . . . We'd play up there, and it was really hot, and the fan is making love to you. And you really had to play, 'cos those people were really hard to please. It was one of the hardest audiences in the South; they hear it all the time. Everybody knows how to play guitar. You went down the street and people are sitting on their porch playing more guitar. That's where I learned to play, really, in Nashville."

Hendrix, Cox, and Lee were living out a low-rent rock and roll fantasy, backing up nationally known artists who came through Nashville and touring on the side. The threesome got its highest-profile gig in late 1962, when they took part in a so-called package tour that included Curtis Mayfield and the Impressions. But Hendrix parted ways with Cox and Lee soon afterward and made his way to Vancouver, where he stayed with his grandmother and hooked up with a local soul group called the Vancouvers. Hendrix's skill was so apparent that

During his Nashville years, Hendrix went on tour as a backup musician for established artists such as Sam Cooke. A dynamic gospel-influenced vocalist, Cooke was responsible for such classic rhythm and blues hits as "You Send Me" and "Bring It on Home to Me."

he rarely had trouble finding work. But he just could not seem to stick with one band. In the spring of 1963 he returned to Nashville but stayed only briefly before hitting the road again. Hendrix wanted to see the world. He would spend the rest of his life chasing sunsets and logging miles with a guitar.

Playing in backup and cover bands, no matter where he traveled, could not completely nourish Hendrix's creative spirit. Since the age of 18 he had been writing poetry, songs, and lyrics, though he had far more confidence in his playing than his singing. (He never really learned to read or score music, despite his band classes.) One untitled verse from his teenage years demonstrates his playfulness with language and imagery and his sense of standing apart from the crowd: "To show how the cats will rap your / scratchings if you're not on into / their latchings / statched at the main crib / Crib on hep cat square / When I just hit this trip / I was laughed for a square."

Back in Nashville, Hendrix hooked up with a package tour featuring Sam Cooke and Jackie Wilson, two leading artists whose styles combined soul music with rhythm and blues. The tour promoter was George Odell, better known as Gorgeous George. Odell was a jack-of-all-trades and had earned his nickname during his days as a professional wrestler. More of a showman than a musician, Odell sported a platinum wig onstage and wore clothes that were even louder than the music. All the same, his band was good enough to back up Cooke and Wilson on tour, and Odell was astute enough to recognize Hendrix's raw talent and offer him a job. Hendrix jumped aboard Odell's tour bus for a ride that would carry him, on and off, through the next two years. He traveled the country with Gorgeous George and played behind some of the top pop acts of the day, including Cooke, Wilson,

Hank Ballard and the Midnighters, the Supremes, and Little Richard.

While on the road, Hendrix encountered some of the guitar heroes who had influenced his own playing. On a visit to Chess Records, home of the Chicago blues, he met Muddy Waters, the first guitarist he ever remembered hearing, and they spent an afternoon talking about guitar and trading secrets. Later in his career, Hendrix incorporated a number of Waters's classic songs into his repertoire, adapting them to his own style.

Hendrix left George Odell's entourage for a spell in late 1963 and went alone to New York. This was a career move: Hendrix thought he would find more opportunities to play music in New York than in Nashville. He also felt the tug of the big city, which promised everything in excess, including a nightlife that spilled into daytime and pulsed to music being played in a thousand halls and clubs. Hendrix's first stop was Harlem, the cultural and spiritual center of New York's African-American community. Harlem bared itself to the visitor in urban extremes: wealth and poverty, beauty and decay, high art in its smoky jazz clubs and life at the lowest rung for the winos and junkies who haunted the streets and alleyways.

Though he was a seasoned traveler, nothing could have prepared Hendrix for this place. Harlem's tangle of grit, menace, attitude, and raw energy was unlike anything the young man from faraway Seattle had ever experienced. Hendrix, as usual, was penniless upon arrival and had to pawn his guitar for food and hotel money. (Later, when he had some cash, he was able to redeem it.) Some nights he had to sleep in an alley or pick through trash cans for food. In the daytime he would hang around recording studios or Harlem clubs like the Palm Café, checking out the local musicians and trying to get himself invited onstage to play with house bands. It was rough going. Despite Hendrix's talents and his impressive résumé, the established players shrugged him off. But he did not allow these experiences to shake his confidence. He entered the talent competition at Harlem's legendary Apollo Theatre one night and won the first prize of $25. It was hardly a fortune, but by winning, Hendrix joined a distinguished list of Apollo Amateur Night champs that included James Brown and Sarah Vaughan.

Hendrix soon found a valuable friend in Fayne Pridgeon, a Harlem woman he met in a club one night. Pridgeon had connections in Harlem's music community, and she introduced Hendrix to club owners and players who could offer him work. In March 1964, Hendrix joined the Isley Brothers, a soul troupe whose hits included the high-energy frat-party standard "Shout." A friend of the Isleys had seen Hendrix performing at the Palm and had introduced him to the group. Hendrix recorded and toured with the Isley Brothers for the next several months. He also played on the group's 1964 single " Testify. "

The Isleys took Hendrix places he had never been, north to Montreal and south to the Caribbean. They also let Hendrix cut loose on stage and play freely; Hendrix was inclined to do so anyway, and the crowds ate it up. He was using these shows to refine his stage presence until he could work an audience into a breathless frenzy, the way he had seen it done by blues guitarists and saxophone players when he was just a face in the crowd. Though the Isleys indulged all his experiments, Hendrix remained as restless as ever. He left the group in Nashville and hooked up with George Odell for another package tour. He later went to Atlanta, where he landed a job with one of rock and roll's early heroes: Little Richard, who was mounting a comeback after spending several years out of the music business.

The Hendrix–Little Richard connection was a brief and stormy one. Little Richard, a flamboyant performer with an electrifying voice and a temper to match, was not the type to share the spotlight with anybody, including the members of his backup band. He was the star; they were hired help. Suddenly, however, he had to deal with an upstart guitarist who went onstage in gaudy clothes and performed flashy guitar tricks for the crowd—Little Richard's crowd. Hendrix's showmanship infuriated the man who was paying his way. In relations with their musicians, the Isley Brothers had believed in democracy; Little Richard was a tyrant. Once, after Hendrix went onstage wearing a frilly ruffled shirt, Little Richard fined him five dollars and demanded that he give up the garment. Not long after, Hendrix quit.

Hendrix went back to New York and joined one of the city's top rhythm and blues club groups, Curtis Knight and the Squires, and embarked with them on a tour of the Northeast. This was a breakthrough gig for Hendrix, who was now enjoying a level of exposure previously unknown to him in the area. He was playing sold-out shows from New York to Boston and finally commanding respect from the members of New York City's rhythm and blues elite. Egged on by Knight and his fellow Squires, Hendrix took long solos, peeling off beautiful blues passages with his strong, graceful fingers, sometimes even flipping the guitar up to his face and playing it with his teeth—a stunt that astounded onlookers.

Work was now plentiful. Hendrix went on to play with Joey Dee and the Starlighters, another New York club-circuit band with a large and loyal following. He also gigged with Curtis King and the Kingpins and then joined Carl Holmes and the Commanders. He even landed in the recording stu-

dio backing up the glamorous film star Jayne Mansfield.

Finally, Hendrix had a little money. He had access to excellent guitars. He was almost making a living playing music, and he was only 23 years old. He had even signed a couple of small recording contracts. But none of it was enough to satisfy him. "I still have my guitar and amp and as long as I have that, no fool can keep me from living," he wrote to his father in a letter dated August 8,

Hendrix's musical career took off in 1965 when he joined Curtis Knight and the Squires. The band played to large audiences throughout the Northeast, and Knight gave Hendrix ample opportunity to showcase his wizardry on the guitar.

1965. "It could be worse than this, but I'm going to keep hustling and scuffling until I get things happening like they're supposed to for me." What he wanted, more than anything, was to play and sing his own songs. He knew he had the guitar craft. He had a head full of ideas. He was not so sure about his voice—particularly after working behind gifted vocalists such as Sam Cooke, Little Richard, and Curtis Knight. But he knew that outside the rhythm and blues milieu, a singer did not have to have a rich, gospel-tutored set of pipes to sound right for a particular song. Hendrix discovered this the moment he heard a young artist from the Midwest named Bob Dylan.

In 1965, Dylan was a trailblazer in the emerging "electric folk" movement that was catching on mostly with white youngsters in the cities and suburbs. It was the sort of music nobody would play in Harlem. Hendrix would have to go downtown to the arty clubs and coffeehouses of Greenwich Village to hear groups that were experimenting with rock, folk, blues, beat poetry, and strange new sounds not yet categorized. Dylan's 1965 album, *Highway 61 Revisited,* with its sparse vocals, poetic lyrics, and freewheeling melodies, piqued Hendrix's interest in the new direction rock and roll was taking. Dylan's voice, which rarely rose above a nasal rasp, also convinced Hendrix that he, too, could sing if he wanted to.

Hendrix finally decided to leave the rhythm and blues circuit and blaze his own trail. He played his last show with Curtis Knight in May 1966 and finished up with Carl Holmes in June. Heading downtown into Greenwich Village, he began turning up at open-microphone nights and getting himself booked into small venues like the Night Owl Café and Café Wha? In the summer of 1966, he formed a four-piece band, came up with the name Jimmy James and the Blue Flames, and shopped the band around to Village club owners. It was like starting from scratch. Hendrix was reaching for a different audience now: the people who cheered him onstage with Curtis Knight or the Isley Brothers did not spend their time in the Village.

In addition to Hendrix, the new band included second guitarist Randy California, a gifted teenage player Jimmy had met at a music store in midtown Manhattan. The names of the bassist and drummer have been forgotten, and they have never stepped forward to share their stories.

Having given up his steady gigs, Hendrix was soon broke and looking to friends for help. He was crashing in lofts with other musicians, some of whom, such as Byrds guitarists David Crosby and Roger McGuinn, would go on to their own fame. Word of Hendrix's guitar prowess spread quickly through the downtown grapevine. Soon he had some of the city's best young musicians coming to hear him or to play alongside him as best they could—Hendrix, fluid in seemingly any style, simply blew away most of his peers. But their admiration could not clothe or feed him.

"When I first met Jimi he was destitute," rock musician John Hammond, Jr., later recalled. "He had even been robbed of his guitar. . . . I was playing at a club called the Gaslight. Across the street was the Café Wha?, a really funky joint. Jimi was playing there, and I went by one night. He was playing some of my songs. . . . He was incredible-looking and seemed pleased to meet me. I asked him how I could help, and he said: 'Get me a gig. Get me out of here!' So I got him a gig at the Café Au Go Go and I worked there with him for a month with Jimi playing lead guitar."

Mingled with the New Yorkers in these bohemian audiences were a few music fans from England who were connected to the so-called British Invasion led by the Beatles and the Rolling

Chas Chandler (center, with bass), shown here during his days with the Animals. After hearing Hendrix play at a Greenwich Village club in 1966, Chandler became the guitarist's manager and convinced him to relocate to England.

Stones. Among them was Chas Chandler, who had played bass in the British group the Animals. At the urging of a friend, Chandler dropped in at Café Wha? on July 5, 1966, and saw Hendrix for the first time.

Once was all he needed. Chandler, as interested in business as he was in music, could hardly believe that this remarkable guitarist was not already signed by a record label or management company. He approached Hendrix and said, "I believe you'll be a sensation in Britain." Hendrix was listening. He asked if Chandler knew Eric Clapton, the revered British electric-blues guitarist. Chandler said he did and promised an introduction if Hendrix came to England. The two huddled in the basement bar for a long time, hammering out the basics of a deal that would bring Hendrix to London, where he would assemble a band to record and play his own songs. Chandler and a business partner back in England would manage Hendrix's career.

It took several weeks to settle everything and to get a copy of Hendrix's birth certificate from Seattle so that he could receive his passport. On September 23, 1966, with the United States drifting toward full-scale war in Vietnam and English bands moving up the American charts, Hendrix and his manager boarded a plane at Kennedy Airport. Now he was flying again, crossing the Atlantic Ocean to London with everything he owned stuffed into a single guitar case. It was like jump school all over again, another leap into the unknown. The bird's-eye view of New York City stretched out below the soaring plane would be Hendrix's last glimpse of home for nearly a year. ☙

4

FIRE

CHAS CHANDLER SPENT the entire flight plotting Hendrix's course through a whirl of pending details: equipment, money, clothes, auditions, a band, studio time, tour dates, press, publicity. But a thornier problem awaited as soon as the two musicians stepped off the plane: British immigration officers. Hendrix had no money, no luggage apart from his guitar case, and no concrete offers of work. Somehow he had to convince the authorities that he was entering the country for some legitimate purpose. His odd clothes and unruly mane of hair did not help his cause.

Chandler did some creative storytelling, and Hendrix was granted a seven-day tourist visa. This was not the ideal way to launch a rock and roll career, but it was better than a return-trip ticket home. Hendrix and Chandler left Heathrow Airport and went immediately to the home of a musician named Zoot Money. Money's place was a meetinghouse for London players; Hendrix walked into a jam session, which he quickly joined. Introductions were made, and Hendrix picked up a guitar. That night he also sat in with some local musicians at a club called the Scotch of St. James, giving the London club crawlers a preview of things to come.

London in 1966 was a city in flux, a faded political center in the post–World War II era but an emerging voice in Western culture, thanks to the

Hendrix in London in 1967, listening to some of his favorite blues records. Having arrived in the British capital only a year earlier as a complete unknown, Hendrix was now an up-and-coming performer widely admired by Britain's rock and roll superstars.

51

rise of British rock bands such as the Yardbirds, the Animals, and the Who. Even with its blue blood thinned by time and events, London clung doggedly to its aristocratic ways. The young Brits who belonged to the city's "mod" scene, shown so vividly in the 1966 film *Blowup,* flaunted their cool like little princes, aloof to anything that happened before dusk. London's youth movement bore only faint resemblance to the spirited hippie culture taking root across the Atlantic.

Chandler put out the word that he had brought home a smashing young guitarist from America, a player who would amaze the blues-rock connoisseurs of the British underground and go on to electrify the world. The British delighted in boosting American artists who were underappreciated or overlooked in their own country. Blues players who found interest and opportunity waning at home, such as Muddy Waters and Mississippi John Hurt, were coaxed to Great Britain, where they could earn good money playing to adoring crowds.

Chandler saw Hendrix doing more than just following in that tradition. Hendrix would cause a sensation. He would blow people's minds. First, though, Hendrix needed a band. Chandler installed Hendrix at the Hyde Park Towers Hotel and went about setting up auditions. Word traveled fast, but players arrived thinking they were vying for a spot with the Animals. Then they saw Hendrix and hardly knew what to expect next.

Chandler and Hendrix had decided to keep the lineup lean: only a bassist and a drummer would fill out the band. Hendrix could sing well enough for rock and roll, and, more important, he could generate more sound with his Fender Stratocaster than most bands with two guitarists.

Noel Redding walked in on the first day of auditions, which were held at a club called Birdland. A guitarist, Redding had played in a handful of British

Soon after his arrival in London, Hendrix hired drummer Mitch Mitchell (left) and bassist Noel Redding and formed the Jimi Hendrix Experience. Though the Experience was to last barely more than three years, it produced some of the most remarkable music in rock and roll history.

bands—none of which, he concluded, was going anywhere. Hendrix and Chandler were intrigued by Redding even before he played a note. He was lean-faced and handsome. With a thicket of frizzy red hair and glasses perched like old-fashioned pince-nez on the end of his aristocratic nose, he looked British yet somehow exotic. It was a look Hendrix and Chandler liked. "I dug his hairstyle," Hendrix later said, "so I asked him to play bass."

Redding agreed. "I'll switch to bass," he said. "I don't see anybody else playing lead guitar with this bloke." He was hired right away. Hendrix's band was now two-thirds complete. All they needed was a drummer.

Mitch Mitchell showed up believing the gig was his if he wanted it. A short, wiry Briton with boyish looks, he knew his way around a drum kit and had already spent much of his life in front of audiences, first as a child actor in the British television series "Jennings at School" and then as a drummer in a series of British pop and swing bands. The last of these was, coincidentally, a group called Georgie Fame and the Blue Flames, which had played a few gigs with the Animals. Mitchell, only 19 years old, was between bands when Chandler called him and encouraged him to stop by. Mitchell was game for anything. He was a cocky little sprite who impressed Hendrix and Chandler with his musical and rhythmic dexterity. He won the job.

Neither Mitchell nor Redding knew quite what to make of the guitarist they were chosen to accompany. Neither had had much contact with black Americans, except for the blues musicians who toured Great Britain. And Hendrix was an enigma—wild looking but quiet, low-key in his treatment of other people but uninhibited, even crazy, with his guitar.

"At the audition it was strange," Mitchell wrote in his autobiography. "I met this black guy with very, very wild hair wearing this Burberry rain-coat. He looked very straight really, apart from the hair. We didn't talk much at first. . . . [Hendrix] was very soft-spoken and gave the impression of being very gentle, almost shy. It was immediately apparent that he was a good guitarist; but at that stage I was more knocked out that he could cover so many different styles as well. You name it he could do it. I think we did 'Have Mercy Babe' first. [Hendrix] didn't really sing, more mumbled along to the music—Chas really had to coax it out of him."

Chandler had quietly worked out Hendrix's visa problems. But there was no time to lounge in London. Chandler and his partner, a former British army soldier named Mike Jeffery, felt they had to move quickly. First of all, Hendrix's band needed a name. Hendrix, Mitchell, Redding, and Chandler sat around a rehearsal space one day, swapping ideas. Somebody tossed out the word *experience.* It had a nice ring. Chandler, meanwhile, was thinking about how Hendrix's name would look in print—on play-bills, posters, record albums, and magazine covers. He started moving letters around and came up with a flashy variation: "Jimi." He remembered the pre-vious discussion, and finally he had it: the Jimi Hendrix Experience. Chandler believed nobody would ever forget this name after they heard Hendrix play.

The Jimi Hendrix Experience played its first gig on October 13, 1966, at a concert hall called Novelty in Evreux, France. It was the first date on a one-week showcase with crooner Johnny Halliday. The trio played a 15-minute set of cover songs, revved up by Hendrix's incendiary licks, Redding's brisk, guitarlike bass lines, and Mitchell's agile drumming, which Hendrix partic-ularly enjoyed. Mitchell treated music like a com-petitive sport; he seemed to relish pushing Hendrix, daring him to match or surpass his own fireworks if he could. The tour ended with a sold-out show at the 14,500-seat L'Olympia in Paris.

Despite the good crowds, reviews of the first Experience dates in France were dismissive. "Bad mixture of James Brown and Chuck Berry," one critic wrote after the Evreux show. Indeed, the band was loose and underrehearsed, having played its first gig barely three weeks after Hendrix came off the plane. Chandler and Hendrix sat down after every show in France and critiqued the performances, looking for ways to sharpen the band's delivery.

But Chandler had more than stagecraft on his mind. The Experience, he knew, could go back to London, make a splash in clubs, and dazzle everybody who saw them—and the whole thing would then expire. The band needed a single. Without a record, there would be no next level for Hendrix, much less a return on Chandler's already considerable investment. He had pawned five of his six guitars to pay for equipment and tour costs. He wanted that single out quickly.

The band made its London debut at a press party and concert organized by Chandler at Bag O' Nails on November 25, two days before Hendrix's 24th birthday. Chandler, meanwhile, booked the group into a studio to record "Hey Joe," a dusty blues number by Tim Rose about a man who kills his girlfriend in a moment of jealous rage and flees to Mexico to escape the law. It was one of the first songs Chandler had ever heard Hendrix play when he walked into Café Wha?

The band also played "Hey Joe" in its British television debut on the program "Ready, Steady, Go!" The performance was broadcast live on December 13. The single hit the record stores three days later and, slowly at first, began to sell and find its way onto the radio.

The Jimi Hendrix Experience prepares for a performance at L'Olympia in Paris, where the band concluded its first tour in 1966. Upon returning to London, Hendrix and his band mates recorded their first hit single, "Hey Joe."

Meanwhile, the Jimi Hendrix Experience was playing club dates at hip London venues like Blaises and Bag O' Nails and attracting a class of people who were more accustomed to being watched than watching: rock stars. The young lions of the British Invasion, who were already conquering America, were now coming to see this American in their midst. Pete Townshend of the Who, Mick Jagger of the Rolling Stones, Paul McCartney of the Beatles, Jeff Beck of the Yardbirds, Eric Clapton of Cream—

Mick Jagger and Keith Richard of the Rolling Stones were among the British rockers who flocked to hear Hendrix during his early London performances. Thoroughly versed in blues-based music, the British were nonetheless astounded by Hendrix's inventive and dynamic guitar playing.

all subjected themselves to the crush of crowds to check out this phenomenal young man who played rock and absolutely authentic blues. They marveled at Hendrix's outrageous playing and expressive, aggressive showmanship on stage. Their presence, in turn, brought the Experience the instant credibility that Chandler sought. With Britain's rock aristocracy giving Hendrix its seal of approval, the record-company executives, radio people, and tour promoters were now looking up and taking notice.

Very quickly, Hendrix and his bandmates were the darlings of the London underground, mingling in the court of British rock royalty and meeting more people than they could count. One night Hendrix ran into his old boss, Little Richard, who cheerfully loaned him $50. Hendrix and Rolling

Stones guitarist Brian Jones became close friends. Jones, like Hendrix, was an experimentalist, drawn to the electric guitar's capacity to produce an endless variety of textures and sounds.

The Experience also caught the eye of the British press. The first write-ups were mixed, sometimes mocking and occasionally racist. "WILD MAN FROM BORNEO" read a headline in the British publication *Disc and Music Echo*. But Chandler relished such reactions: the more the press gasped at this "wild man" with the kinky hair and noisy guitar, the more British youths would tune in and listen.

Hendrix was also creating a look for himself built on his taste for Old World finery. He would go onstage in a 19th-century cavalry jacket or stride about London like some princely modern-day Mozart in ruffles and shades. He took an apartment, a small flat above a pub in London's Montagu Square, covered the windows with heavy curtains, and painted the walls black. He turned the space into a darkened salon, a little baroque cocoon. Through his window he could see the rooftops of London, a city that looked and felt nothing like Seattle, except perhaps for the clouds and steady rain.

The Experience's early live shows thrived on disarray and on the band's ability to skirt a collapse in midflight, with Hendrix somehow holding it all together and simultaneously pushing the music outward into places nobody had gone before. He brandished his guitar like an acetylene torch, slicing fresh contours into a sonic wall. The sound moved and flowed to currents seemingly directed by Hendrix's hands, twisting into shapes that split, subdivided, merged, and then reconfigured—like echoes—into something familiar but always new.

Chandler's partner, Mike Jeffery, went to the United States and, touting the success of "Hey

Joe," returned to Britain in January 1967 having pulled off a coup: a U.S. record deal. Warner Bros. agreed to give the Experience a $150,000 advance—an unheard-of amount of money for a little-known band. Jeffery, who had managed the Animals and (Chandler suspected) probably robbed them blind, was nothing if not persuasive.

"Hey Joe" peaked at number four on the British charts in February. It was time for another single. The Experience went back into the studio to record "Purple Haze." Hendrix wrote the tune—built around a distinctive two-note stomp with spacey guitar breaks—in the dressing room of the Upper Cut Club. Originally a 20-minute composition subtitled "Jesus Saved," the song had to be drastically cut for commercial reasons, and Hendrix always felt that the spiritual message of the lyrics was lost in the process. "Purple Haze" reached stores and radio stations on March 17, while "Hey Joe" was still on the charts. The new single climbed to the top five in a fraction of the time it had taken the first song to peak.

The Jimi Hendrix Experience now had two songs in play and was packing concert halls across the United Kingdom as well as Germany, France, Belgium, and the Netherlands. They slipped into the studio between shows, putting Hendrix's songs on tape whenever time allowed.

The Experience joined a monthlong British tour with Cat Stevens, the Walker Brothers, and Engelbert Humperdinck. Chandler and Hendrix were determined to make the band stand out on opening night. They had spent hours working out stage routines, body language, timing of song introductions, even the suggestive way Hendrix stroked the neck and body of his guitar—all the things that made proper British observers cringe. Now they wanted to raise the theatrical pitch another notch. The opportunity came on the tour's second night.

Hendrix's exuberance helped make the Experience a major concert attraction throughout Western Europe. However, Hendrix began to feel that some fans cared little about the music and were mainly interested in seeing him do something outrageous onstage.

London's Finsbury Park Astoria concert hall was jammed with eager spectators on March 31, 1967, as the Experience galloped through a brisk set. When the band finished "Fire," a new song, Hendrix went into his act. He tossed his Fender Stratocaster to the floor of the stage and, to the audience's surprise, produced a tin of lighter fluid. Dropping to his knees, he splashed the guitar with butane, pulled out a lighter, and held the flame to his guitar. Nothing happened. Hendrix tried again. And again. Then, on the fourth try, a column of flame leaped straight up from the stage floor. The crowd gasped. Hendrix's guitar was burning. Finsbury Park went berserk.

The theater's managers were enraged by Hendrix's stunt, and the other acts were angry at being upstaged. There was talk of dropping the Experience from the tour. British newspapers were already complaining about Hendrix's stage demeanor. "His movements were far too suggestive for an audience mostly in the 14–18 age group," the *Lincolnshire Chronicle* fretted. But the tour promoters also knew that controversy boosted receipts at the box office. Hendrix was a smash. He was the one that people were coming to see.

In May, the Jimi Hendrix Experience released its third single, a dreamy, spartan ballad called "The Wind Cries Mary." Hendrix wrote it after a heated argument with his first girlfriend in London, Kathy Etchingham, although some commentators consider the song an ode to his mother, Lucille. Later that month, the group released its first full-length album, *Are You Experienced?* This 11-song tour through Hendrix's musical psyche veered from baroque ("Manic Depression") to blues ("Red House"), its stylistic wanderings always yanked back to earth by the ferocity of the guitar, bass, and drums.

The album shot up to number three in Britain, two notches below the top spot occupied by the Beatles' *Sgt. Pepper's Lonely Hearts Club Band.* Europe could not get enough of Hendrix. Crowds crammed concert halls that tour promoters had deliberately overbooked to watch him play, writhe, smash his guitar through his amplifier, and walk offstage with his shattered equipment still screeching through loudspeakers. Hendrix began to find the response disconcerting. He enjoyed theatrics; they could be as expressive as his guitar work. But he also had begun to notice that he could step onstage and play well or play badly, and nobody seemed to notice either way. Whatever he served, the crowds would eat it up. They just wanted Hendrix to live up to his hype.

The Experience conquered Europe in short order, and the speed of their ascent convinced Chandler and Jeffery that bigger things were coming. Success in Europe only went so far; even with Hendrix topping British charts, the band was still making peanuts playing live. The biggest untapped market lay before them. For Hendrix to establish himself as a solo artist and a star, he had to go home.

Chandler and Jeffery were already planning the Experience's first trip to America; they had lined up dates at the Fillmore West in San Francisco, run by the dynamic rock impresario Bill Graham. San Francisco and Los Angeles were the spawning grounds for an emerging music scene led by bands like Buffalo Springfield, Jefferson Airplane, and the Grateful Dead. Several promoters wanted to show off California's homegrown talent and establish the West Coast as a new music capital on the order of Nashville or Detroit. One of them, John Phillips of the Mamas and the Papas, was organizing a benefit concert in Monterey, halfway between San Francisco and Los Angeles. The Monterey International Pop Festival was a gamble, a pilot project for the outdoor rock-show spectaculars that would become a mainstay of the industry.

Phillips envisioned an unprecedented collection of all-star talent, and the biggest challenge was booking bands. The Beatles were too busy; the Rolling Stones were tied up with a court battle; the Beach Boys signed up but then backed out. But Paul McCartney of the Beatles told Phillips to check out an American expatriate living in Britain, a guitarist named Jimi Hendrix. Phillips was game. He called Chas Chandler in England, and the two struck a deal. The Jimi Hendrix Experience would make its U.S. debut not in a dark, smoke-filled club, but in front of several thousand people on a spring day in California. With the stakes raised so high, Hendrix's homecoming would either be a smash or a swan dive. ♨

5

EXERIENCE

HENDRIX HAD LEFT New York with a guitar and some clothes; he returned with a band and a crew. He and his friends spent two days changing hotels and knocking around Hendrix's old haunts in Harlem and the Village. From New York, they flew to San Francisco and took a charter flight to Monterey.

The Monterey International Pop Festival, held June 16–18, boasted 31 different acts, including Booker T and the MG's, Simon and Garfunkel, Laura Nyro, the Grateful Dead, Hugh Masekela, Ravi Shankar, Canned Heat, Dionne Warwick, Country Joe and the Fish, Eric Burdon and the Animals (minus Chandler), the Who, and the Jimi Hendrix Experience. Monterey Pop, as it came to be known, blossomed into a counterculture bazaar, drawing hippies, flower children, Hell's Angels, and, of course, the Warner Bros. record executives coming to see the guitarist they had signed for $150,000. Some 30,000 people came to Monterey for the festival; only a fraction of that number could squeeze into the arena.

Hendrix was scheduled to play Sunday night, along with the Grateful Dead and the Who. He spent Friday and Saturday partying, meeting people, and generally doing anything that struck his fancy. On the morning of his performance, he sat down outside his motel room with several guitars

Hendrix appears in a pensive mood in a take from Don Pennebaker's Monterey Pop, *a film record of the 1967 California festival. Hendrix's dazzling performance at Monterey established him as a major force on the American music scene.*

and a paint kit and decorated his instruments like Easter eggs.

On Sunday, with showtime approaching, an argument broke out between Hendrix and guitarist Pete Townshend of the Who. Townshend was demanding that the Who play first; he had followed Hendrix once before, several months back on a double bill in England, and did not want to repeat the experience. The problem was stylistic: Hendrix tended to finish up a set the same way Townshend did, by smashing guitars and trashing the stage. Townshend was sure he would look like an idiot at Monterey if he played wrecking ball after the crowd had already seen that routine. There was no way he would play behind the Experience. Hendrix argued back but eventually gave in; he was pleased just to be on the bill.

Townshend, true to form, pulled his gear down around him. The carnage prompted Peter Tork of the Monkees, a hugely popular teenybopper band, to walk onstage and plead with everybody to behave. The Grateful Dead played next, and the Experience followed. Hendrix opened the set with a salute to one of the great blues artists who had inspired him, playing Howlin' Wolf's "Killing Floor." The band followed with "Foxy Lady," the bump-and-grind number that starts *Are You Experienced?*

Hendrix treated the overflow audience to an energetic, inspired show, charging through his riotous stage act with unrestrained joy. He was home again, and he loved it. He held his guitar in every imaginable position. He toyed with feedback, bending the banshee notes pouring from his Marshall amplifiers like an operatic tenor. Then he churned out the chords of another song he loved: Bob Dylan's "Like a Rollin' Stone." The crowd, taken with this homage to one of their heroes, responded with enthusiasm. Cries of "Jimi! Jimi!"

floated toward the stage. The Experience pushed onward: "Rock Me Baby," "Hey Joe," "Can You See Me," "The Wind Cries Mary," "Purple Haze."

The set was nearly finished. "I could sit up here all night and say, thank you. . . . I just want to grab you, man," Hendrix told a crowd that was now totally his. "But dig, I just can't do that. So what I wanna do, I'm gonna sacrifice something here that I really love, okay. . . . Don't think I'm silly

Pete Townshend of the Who performs during the late 1960s. At the Monterey Pop Festival, Townshend insisted on performing ahead of the Experience, believing that anyone following Hendrix would look tame by comparison.

doing this, 'cause I don't think I'm losing my mind. . . . There's nothing more I can do than this."

With a feedback howl, he opened "Wild Thing," a three-chord rock stomp by a British band called the Troggs. Hendrix tore the song up and made it his own. It ended in a welter of crashing, cascading sound as guitar, bass, and drum notes rippled through the air like fireworks. The crowd had already seen Townshend's demolition act, but Hendrix was unconcerned. With the song still ringing, out came the lighter fluid and matches. Flames enveloped the hand-painted guitar. Hendrix grabbed it by the neck and smashed it while it burned, and wild, tortured sounds screamed through the arena's loudspeakers. Finally, Hendrix threw the blackened, splintered pieces of his Stratocaster into the crowd. The sacrifice was done.

Whatever else Hendrix achieved that night, he literally burned his image into the minds of all those at Monterey. Reviewers were divided: "[Hendrix] graduated from rumor to legend," said one, whereas another called the performance "a vulgar parody of rock theatrics." The executives from Warner Bros. were perplexed and concerned. They had footed some of the bill for the concert as a promotional gambit and watched their new artist trash the equipment they had paid for. They were now inclined to proceed more cautiously with Hendrix.

But the torch was burning. Both the crowd and the musicians backstage were blown away by Hendrix's performance. "You killed them, man!" Hugh Masekela crowed in his singsong South African accent. "You killed them!" echoed a beaming Brian Jones, who had come from England just to see Hendrix play. Nobody was happier than Bill Graham, who had booked the Experience for six nights at the Fillmore West.

Hendrix spent the evening at the Laurel Canyon home of musician Stephen Stills, where he was immediately embraced by America's rock and roll elite. What had happened in Britain was now threatening to happen again, but on a gargantuan scale. A breakthrough in America would dwarf anything Hendrix had done overseas. So far, he was fulfilling Chandler's fondest hopes.

By the time Hendrix got to San Francisco, word of his triumph at Monterey had traveled over the West Coast grapevine, with some help from Graham, who was building a coast-to-coast business on his ability to promote rock. Crowds jammed the Fillmore West for five nights in a row, filling the hall for a total of 10 shows. On the sixth day, Sunday, June 25, 1967, the Experience played a free concert in Golden Gate Park on the back of a flatbed truck and did one more Fillmore show before heading to Los Angeles. Graham gave the Experience a $2,000 bonus and presented everybody with engraved watches before they left.

Chandler and Jeffery, meanwhile, were scrambling to line up more gigs. The Experience had come to America with only Monterey and the Fillmore West on its calendar. Everything from that point on was improvised, which probably explains what happened next.

Jeffery had run off to New York. It was rapidly becoming his trademark to disappear and then resurface, like a diver snorkeling for loot in a sunken galley, with some breathtaking prize. And sure enough, when he called Chandler, Jeffery had big news: he had just landed the Experience a spot on a nationwide tour with one of America's hottest bands, the Monkees.

For a second, Chandler could not breathe. "Are you out of your ——— mind?" he shouted into the phone.

Hendrix performs one of his most memorable stage feats, setting fire to his guitar at the end of his set. At Monterey, his uninhibited performance of "Wild Thing," climaxed by the smashing and burning of his instrument, was remembered by many fans as the concert's most exciting event.

Chandler was aghast. His business partner had just contracted the flamboyant, provocative Jimi Hendrix to open for a band whose core audience slept in pajamas. Chandler suddenly saw everything he had worked for crashing in a laughable heap. Hendrix on a bill with the Monkees would become a joke.

Jeffery saw things differently. Here was a chance for exposure, he reasoned; the Monkees were the most popular band in the country behind the Beatles. They had their own television show, and because they wanted to be taken seriously by the rock community, they eagerly agreed to bring Hendrix aboard. Chandler flew to New York to tell Jeffery this tour would be a disaster and that he would have no part of it. Hendrix, for his part, was as furious as Chandler. He hated the Monkees. But the papers were signed. It was too late to back out now.

The Monkees' television production company, Screen Gems, was paying for the tour, which company executives basically viewed as a way to promote the TV show. In this endeavor, Screen Gems spared no expense. The Monkees—Peter Tork, Davey Jones, Mike Nesmith, and Mickey Dolenz—traveled in their own plane, and the Experience flew with them. The musicians stayed in posh hotels, such as the Waldorf-Astoria in New York, with whole floors closed off for their exclusive use. There were lavish parties and boat cruises—whatever it took to keep the Monkees in the public eye.

As for the gigs, Hendrix was slated to play a 25-minute set—a warm-up routine, basically—with the house lights still up and youngsters still filing into their seats, parents in tow. A sullen Hendrix would greet the crowd with an attention-getting blast from his guitar, volume cranked, the signal going off like an air raid in his listeners' little ears. A few youngsters seemed to get a charge from the mayhem, but others were frightened by it. Parents who had brought their children to hear "Pleasant Valley Sunday" and other Monkees trifles were aghast.

After several engagements, even Jeffery could see that he had made a mistake. He approached tour promoter Dick Clark—host of the squeaky-clean teen dance show "American Bandstand"—and persuaded Clark that Hendrix and the Monkees were a disastrous combination. But Clark and Jeffery agreed that the Monkees would look foolish if their opening act simply bailed out on them; some sort of cover story was needed. The Hendrix camp came up with an idea and issued a press release saying the Experience was being dropped because an influential women's organization, the Daughters of the American Revolution (DAR), found Hendrix's theatrics vulgar, outrageous, and plainly unsuitable for children. The story sounded plausible; indeed, the thought of Hendrix scandalizing a group of prim, conservative, elderly white women with his oversexed stage act was too wickedly delightful to resist. None of the publications that ran with the press release even bothered to call the DAR for confirmation.

Hendrix played the last of eight Monkees dates on July 16, 1967, at Forest Hills Stadium in Queens, New York, ending one of the daffiest partnerships in rock and roll history. This was the sort of fiasco that could only have happened in rock's formative years, before the rise of sophisticated test-marketing, focus groups, and radio "formats" that carefully segregate groups like the Experience (hard rock) and the Monkees (Top 40). "We decided it was just the wrong audience," Hendrix told the London publication *New Music Express*. "I think they're replacing me with Mickey Mouse."

Meanwhile, Warner Bros. was preparing to release a U.S. version of *Are You Experienced?* that would include three songs omitted from the

European edition of the album ("Purple Haze," "Hey Joe," and "The Wind Cries Mary"). The Warner executives were dubious about the album's prospects, but they had already invested in Hendrix, and they felt obliged to try. *Are You Experienced?* debuted in August and entered *Billboard* magazine's Top 200 chart at 190. The album would spend the next 106 weeks on the chart, peaking at number five.

After leaving the Monkees tour, the Experience played in New York; Washington, D.C.; Michigan;

Perhaps the most bizarre episode in Hendrix's career was the Experience's touring partnership with the Monkees in 1967. The alliance between the wildly mismatched bands dissolved after only eight concert dates.

and California, leapfrogging around the country as gigs presented themselves. They returned to England on August 21, 1967. The band's two months in America had fallen short of a triumph; money was still tight, and not every show had gone as magnificently as Monterey. But there was no denying that the Jimi Hendrix Experience had made an impression. They would be back.

The group spent the rest of 1967 in Europe. They toured, played for radio and television, and recorded tracks for a second album. *Axis: Bold as Love* was released in England on December 1, 1967, four days after Hendrix's 25th birthday. Though he was often on the road in Europe, Hendrix spent as much time as he could in London, where he had friends and a community of people—musicians—to which he truly belonged. But still he kept his distance, as he had done all his life, giving more of himself onstage than he did privately. "I don't think anybody knew him," road manager Gerry Stickells later recalled.

The Jimi Hendrix Experience now topped the bill everywhere they went. But as splendidly as things were going, something familiar was stealing over Hendrix, a sensation he knew too well. His old restlessness began to surface again. Touring was beginning to feel like a drag, a necessity that got in the way of songwriting and recording. Even the recording studio could be frustrating because there was never enough time to get the sounds just right; the tour bus was always idling outside, waiting for him to get aboard. On the road the crowds began to look the same, no matter what their enthusiasm. Hendrix sometimes forgot what city he was in, which was not surprising; in 1967, the Experience played a total of 255 shows.

"I'd like to take a six-month break," Hendrix told Britain's *Melody Maker* magazine in an interview published on December 23. "I'm tired of trying to write stuff and finding I can't." But good things were still happening. The band was sharp. Crowds showered Hendrix with affection, and he rewarded them with his inspired playing. The rock world held him in awe. *Melody Maker* had voted Hendrix the world's best musician in September. And *Axis: Bold as Love* drew uniformly smashing reviews; there would be no dreaded "sophomore slump" for Hendrix. On New Year's Eve, he attended a party at the Speakeasy in London and led a spirited, 30-minute jam of "Auld Lang Syne." ♫

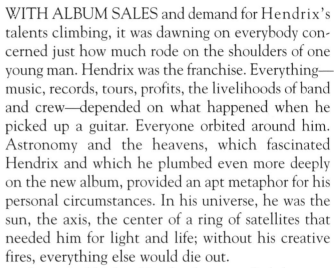

6

PURPLE HAZE

WITH ALBUM SALES and demand for Hendrix's talents climbing, it was dawning on everybody concerned just how much rode on the shoulders of one young man. Hendrix was the franchise. Everything—music, records, tours, profits, the livelihoods of band and crew—depended on what happened when he picked up a guitar. Everyone orbited around him. Astronomy and the heavens, which fascinated Hendrix and which he plumbed even more deeply on the new album, provided an apt metaphor for his personal circumstances. In his universe, he was the sun, the axis, the center of a ring of satellites that needed him for light and life; without his creative fires, everything else would die out.

It is possible that Hendrix began to feel the pressure of his situation. On January 3, 1968, in Göteborg, Sweden, after downing a quantity of whiskey and beer, Hendrix destroyed his hotel room. He also thrust one of his valuable hands through a windowpane and scuffled with the police officers who came to arrest him. Hendrix's passport was impounded, and he spent the night in jail nursing a badly cut

This upbeat photo of the Jimi Hendrix Experience reflects the band's extraordinary success during 1967 and 1968; during this time they were almost continually on tour, shattering box-office records wherever they went.

right hand and recalling his teenage trip through juvenile detention. When Chandler visited, Hendrix said he did not remember what he had done but would gladly pay for any damage. Police fines and hotel expenses wiped out most of the band's income from the Swedish dates. Hendrix later relived the episode in "My Friend," a song he recorded that spring in New York.

The Experience finished its second European tour at L'Olympia in Paris, where the group had opened for Johnny Halliday and the Walker Brothers 15 months earlier. Every date was becoming an exercise in dramatic perspective. Venues that once booked Hendrix as a warm-up act were now trumpeting the Experience with posters and playbills done up in a riot of psychedelic colors. Gigs that brought minimal fees a year earlier were now bringing in thousands of dollars.

On February 10, 1968, *Axis: Bold as Love*, already flying off the shelves in Britain, appeared in U.S. record stores. The album entered the charts in 140th place, reached the top 20 within three weeks, and climbed to number three in the course of a 53-week stay. In contrast to the nonstop rocket ride of *Are You Experienced?, Axis* was filled with dreamy, metaphysical blues steeped in Indian mythology and drenched in lush noise conjured by Hendrix and his studio collaborator, an inventive young engineer from South Africa named Eddie Kramer. Colors bled beautifully through waterfall ballads like "Little Wing" and "Castles Made of Sand." Hendrix also blended multiple instruments—harpsichord, flute, and glockenspiel—with special effects and backward-recorded guitar to create a sensory bath in full stereo. Even by the soaring standard of creativity in new music, *Axis* set Hendrix apart. He simply sounded like nobody else.

The day after the U.S. release of *Axis,* Hendrix arrived in Seattle. He had not been home since

In 1968, Hendrix returned to Seattle for a tour date and was reunited with his family. Here he poses for a photo with his brother, Leon, his father, and his stepsister, Janie.

The Black Elvis

BY FRANK SIMPSON

NEW YORK, Monday. — The somewhat staid New York Times calls him "a black Elvis." The hippy-oriented Los Angeles Free Press gets a little more ecstatic: "He's an electric religion . . . in a cataclysmic-volcanic-organism finale, we fell back limp in our seats, stunned and numbed."

This, plus sell-out audiences and even a gang of teenage ticket forgers, is the reaction that the Jimi Hendrix Experience gets from its current American tour.

Now, mid tour, Jimi Hendrix has four days off — and needs them. He's relaxing in his hotel room in New York after being thrown out of his first hotel— "must have thought I was an Indian," he says.

This article from Melody Maker *magazine sums up Hendrix's impact on the world of rock and roll during 1968.*

1964, and his family had heard next to nothing from him since he first went abroad. But he had called from Europe in early 1968 to say he would be passing through. His father and brother were at the airport to greet him, along with his new stepmother, Ayako, and her daughter Janie.

Hendrix played at Seattle's Center Arena on February 12 with his family smiling up at him from the front row. Early the next morning, February 13, Hendrix arrived at his alma mater, Garfield High School, for a hastily arranged ceremony. He was supposed to receive an honorary diploma and the key to the city, but the planners of the event had botched most of the details: there was no diploma and no key. Hendrix shuffled awkwardly behind a microphone in the school gym, surrounded by local officials and his family. He fielded a few questions from the students, who clearly had no idea who he was. Then he left. The band flew to Los Angeles that day for its next concert.

The Experience tour became a revival locomotive, barreling across the continent and stopping where it chose, with Hendrix preaching new rock gospel in cities and towns, and Mitchell and Redding flanking him onstage like wings in a trinity. Everything was rising—crowd counts, money, decibel levels, the madness onstage. Hendrix slipped completely into this whirl, which took everything he had to give and never stopped.

Everything fed the success machine. Arena crowds topped 15,000. Everywhere the band went, a trail of shattered records for gate receipts followed. Sales of *Are You Experienced?* shot past the million mark. Newspapers shouted Hendrix's praises. Day after day, his songs filled the airwaves. The New York Times called Hendrix "the black Elvis." *Rolling Stone* gave him its "Great Balls of Fire" award. Britain's Disc and Music Echo, which had once labeled Hendrix "Wild Man from Borneo," now called him "World's Top Musician." "They are the same people who first laughed," Hendrix reflected. "They sat behind their typewriters rubbing their bellies. Now they have turned 'understanding.' I don't think they understand my songs. They live in a different world."

Hendrix was now living like his grandmother Nora, the classic vaudevillian with no home but the road, but in circumstances exaggerated to cosmic extremes. By now it felt as if he had played for a million people and traveled a million miles.

The life had its moments. Hendrix, always shy offstage, found it easier than ever to meet women. Like everybody else, they sought him out. It seemed as though Hendrix was never alone. Friends, groupies, and hangers-on kept him company. Bandmates, roadies, managers, publicists, and lawyers protected the business side, which got bigger by the day. "As far as Hendrix's popularity was concerned, it was like a snowball running down a hill," Chandler later said. "I'd never seen anything like it. From September '67 to July '68 he was enormous."

But the pace and the perpetual dislocation were exhausting. There was a predictable routine—travel, play, travel, play—but nothing felt ordered inside that routine. Life was a relentless barrage of people, places, and appointments made by somebody else, a steady diet of airplane flights, strange hotel rooms, and erratic sleep. And the constant collision of onstage highs and postshow crashes made it very easy for a young musician to smooth the rough edges, seek inspiration, or just hide away by using drugs.

Hendrix and his friends were as familiar as any young rockers with the drug culture that was, for the musician, part of the identity and part of the scene. Like many other performers, he popped his way through the rock and roll medicine cabinet of

In a rare solitary moment, Hendrix waits for his luggage after arriving in Zurich, Switzerland, where he was scheduled to perform two concerts in May 1968.

This striking photo of Mitchell, Hendrix, and Redding conveys the tension that began to afflict the trio at the height of their fame. Eventually, the friction between Redding and Hendrix grew so great that the two used separate dressing rooms.

uppers and downers when he needed help coping with his crushing performance schedule. Jeffery was notorious for overbooking the band; during a three-year period, they played a staggering total of 550 concerts.

Drug use in the music world was far from harmless. Eric Clapton, for example, had become addicted to heroin, and Beatles manager Brian Epstein

had died of an overdose. But nobody stopped to reflect on these catastrophes for too long; people were too busy getting to the next gig, partying, living the life.

With so much daily chaos, tensions were bound to rise. One night, in the middle of a show at the Xavier University field house in Cincinnati, Ohio, Hendrix's amplifiers started picking up the signal of the nearby campus radio station. The amps went haywire. Hendrix could not keep the radio chatter from bleeding through his speakers without shutting off the amps. So he walked offstage after four songs and never came back.

In general, equipment was a chronic headache for the Experience. Hendrix played so loud and pushed his gear so hard in search of his ideal sound that scores of amplifiers just blew their tubes. The Experience literally left a trail of broken guitars and blown amps across America.

Meanwhile, Redding and Hendrix had been feuding ever since the recording of *Axis: Bold as Love.* They became so estranged that they even used separate dressing rooms while on tour. The bassist had chafed at Hendrix's slow, deliberate style of sorting through songs in the studio, which forced Redding to sit around for hours, waiting to be told what to play. (Mitchell seemed less bothered by the drill.) Money was another issue. Despite the sold-out concerts and the soaring album sales, the band always seemed to live from hand to mouth, a state of affairs bitterly resented by Redding and Mitchell. Hendrix, who loaned money freely to anyone who needed it, had little interest in finances and mainly concerned himself with his music. "I'm so bad when it comes to money," he once said. "I force myself to save it by not knowing when it's around and not being able to get it any time I want."

Between February and April, the Experience tour went through Washington, California, Texas, Colorado, Illinois, Wisconsin, Michigan, Maine, Massachusetts, Rhode Island, Pennsylvania, Canada, Connecticut, Delaware, Ohio, and Washington, D.C.—49 performances in 70 days, including dates at smaller halls where they played twice a night, 60 to 75 minutes a show. Hendrix and his band were traveling through a country filled with ferment and political turmoil. U.S. military

involvement in Vietnam was at its peak, and protests against the war, especially on the nation's college campuses, were reaching fever pitch. Then, on April 4, 1968, the Reverend Martin Luther King, Jr., the apostle of the black civil rights movement in America, was shot and killed by a sniper in Memphis, Tennessee. On that evening Hendrix was slated to do two shows at the Civic Dome in Virginia Beach, Virginia. He completed the first show, but after the news of King's assassination spread, the second show was canceled.

The Reverend Martin Luther King, Jr., leads a civil rights march in Detroit, Michigan, in 1963. During the turmoil following King's assassination in 1968, Hendrix was pressed to comment on political and racial matters, but he preferred to express his feelings through music.

Though Hendrix was sometimes criticized for his lack of political involvement, he often contributed to charitable causes. Here he enjoys a laugh with folksinger Joan Baez before appearing at a 1968 concert that raised funds for victims of a civil war in the African nation of Nigeria.

Reporters often asked Hendrix about racism, civil rights, poverty, and the riots that ravaged black neighborhoods in Los Angeles, Detroit, and other cities following Dr. King's assassination. Hendrix felt deeply about these events, but he preferred to express himself in music rather than making political statements. "Talking isn't really my scene," he told one interviewer. "Playing is."

Hendrix was drawn deeper and deeper into the political upheavals of the time, whether he liked it or not. The young people who were protesting the Vietnam War by marching, burning their draft cards, and slipping flowers in the barrels of National Guardsmen's rifles saw themselves as part of an uprising—peace soldiers in a revolution of consciousness. They believed in the spiritual power of music, and they conducted their revolution to the sound of Jefferson Airplane, the Doors, the Grateful Dead, Neil Young, Arlo Guthrie, and Jimi Hendrix. On the other side of the divide, the authorities in state and local governments tended to view rock music and its fans as part of a growing nationwide problem, linking the music to violence, drug use, disrespect for authority, and general lawlessness. Hendrix could not insulate himself completely from these conflicts. In June, he attended a benefit at Madison Square Garden for the Martin Luther King Memorial Fund and wrote the fund a $5,000 check to help carry on the struggle for civil rights.

In April, the Experience had pulled into New York to start recording the group's third album. Mitchell, Redding, and Hendrix ensconced themselves in hotel rooms around the city and converged on a Manhattan recording studio called the Record Plant. Hendrix had strong ideas about the new album and took a firmer hand in its making, often over the objections of Chandler, who worried about the cost of studio time and questioned the soundness of Hendrix's thinking. Hendrix was aiming for a major opus, a record that combined the best aspects of the previous albums with a renewed commitment to getting every detail right. His ambition was costing Chandler and the band's sponsors a fortune in studio time. But time after time, Chandler's objections were overruled.

The sessions for the new album turned the Record Plant into a vast living room, with friends, strangers, and other musicians dropping by in a never-ending pilgrimage to see Hendrix, feed him drugs, jam and record with him, or just hang out. Hendrix seemed to enjoy the ambience, but it was driving everybody else crazy. "There was a dreadful atmosphere in the studio," Chandler later claimed. "There were so many people hanging around him, he couldn't be himself. We had an argument about it and he said, 'Okay, no more.' Then someone would turn up at the studio with a bag of goodies and pour some more down his throat. . . . Things began to deteriorate."

Still, the album was progressing, track by track. Hendrix had a head full of songs; so many, it seemed, he could not get them on tape fast enough. The band was putting together enough material for two albums. Mitchell and Redding, however, were increasingly discontented. They missed England. The Experience had played only one concert in Great Britain in all of 1968, at the Woburn Music Festival in July. Otherwise, the band spent the year touring the United States, recording in New York, and jetting back to Europe for spot performances in Italy and Spain.

Redding was also frustrated by Hendrix's apparent lack of interest in his songs. Redding was a songwriter and singer in addition to playing guitar and bass, and he wanted Hendrix to make room on the new album for one of his tunes. After some prodding, Hendrix finally agreed to include Redding's straight-ahead rocker "Little Miss Strange."

In September, the Experience released a single, "All Along the Watchtower," a Bob Dylan song that Hendrix had heard one night at a party. Hendrix took Dylan's spare acoustic version and transformed it into an electric tour de force with a guitar solo that is considered one of the most exquisite he ever played. The Dylan tune appeared on the new Hendrix album, *Electric Ladyland,* which hit the streets October 5, 1968, in England and 11 days later in the United States. It was a double LP, containing a whopping 17 songs on four sides, and because of the added cost, it was not the ideal formula for a hit. But *Electric Ladyland* rocketed to the top of the U.S. charts all the same. Hendrix had his first number-one record.

Like its predecessors, the album was an eclectic smash, fusing rock, funk, and blues with classical flourishes and jazz sounds. From the soaring grace of "All Along the Watchtower" to the street-corner funk of "Crosstown Traffic" to the eerie, shaman-like dirge of "Voodoo Chile (Slight Return)," Hendrix showed he had few if any peers in his ability to merge sounds and styles into an electrifying whole. "Yeah, that whole LP means so much, you know," Hendrix told an interviewer. "It wasn't just slopped together. Every little thing that you hear on there means something, you know. It's no game that we're playing, trying to blow the public's mind or so forth. It's part of us."

The success of the album was a spectacular end to a hectic, chaotic year, and to the world outside Hendrix's circle, it must have portended an even better year to come. But Hendrix's determination to fulfill his own vision in *Electric Ladyland* had its price: Chas Chandler severed his business ties with Hendrix that summer and left New York, feeling that his counsel was no longer wanted. The man who had launched Hendrix's career was now leaving it to others. Chandler's departure was the first major break by anybody in Hendrix's London circle. There were more changes to come. ☙

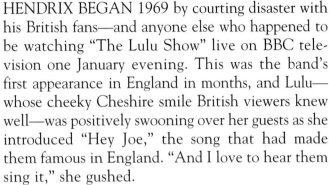

7

POP SLAVERY

HENDRIX BEGAN 1969 by courting disaster with his British fans—and anyone else who happened to be watching "The Lulu Show" live on BBC television one January evening. This was the band's first appearance in England in months, and Lulu—whose cheeky Cheshire smile British viewers knew well—was positively swooning over her guests as she introduced "Hey Joe," the song that had made them famous in England. "And I love to hear them sing it," she gushed.

Hendrix had other ideas. The Experience had gotten about 15 seconds into "Hey Joe" when Hendrix suddenly stopped and coolly announced that it was time to salute Eric Clapton and his recently disbanded group, Cream. With that, the Experience broke into Cream's "Sunshine of Your Love." Lulu, looking baffled, tried to smile her way through this unscripted adventure. But the show's producer was beside himself, waving madly and trying to get Hendrix to stop. The broadcast ended with Hendrix playing right through the credits.

Hendrix was still everybody's shy sweetheart. But his hijacking of "The Lulu Show" showed that

The Jimi Hendrix Experience performs at an informal outdoor concert in San Francisco. As the pressures of touring grew ever greater, Hendrix took more and more pleasure in playing for small audiences; he especially enjoyed informal jam sessions with fellow musicians in small clubs.

he had developed a willful streak that could cause any given performance to take a playful, sullen, or even hostile turn. For Hendrix, the pressure to keep the success machine running threatened to suck the joy and satisfaction out of the thing he loved most: playing. Everybody seemed to have opinions, expectations, and instructions about what he should play and how he should act onstage. Hendrix called this "pop slavery." So he kept his love of performing and his sense of humor intact by throwing curves at his audience. But when his humor failed him, frustration soured into contempt: Hendrix, on some nights, would simply stand behind the microphone, muttering insults under his breath. He sometimes refused to play the crowd-pleasing hits everybody had come to hear.

Controversy over the packaging of *Electric Ladyland* was not helping Hendrix's disposition. The double album opened to reveal a gaggle of young women lounging in the nude like harem inmates in some erotic fantasy. Hendrix was catching flak in the press for the record company's choice of imagery. Coupled with the constant comments about his provocative stage antics, the criticism made him irritable and self-conscious. "I didn't have nothing to do with that stupid LP cover they released and I don't even want to talk about it," he snapped at an interviewer in Philadelphia.

In February 1969, the influential magazine *Rolling Stone* named Hendrix Performer of the Year for 1968. But the irony of that laurel began to surface in his live appearances, which grew more erratic as the new year progressed. Hendrix—under pressure to perform, to record, to earn money, to be everybody's friend—was having trouble with the multiple demands. And the strain registered onstage. He could wreck an evening for one paying crowd with sloppy, grudging guitar work and half-hearted singing, then play brilliantly the next night.

Audiences never knew which Hendrix would show up, but they came to see him anyway. Hendrix hated that more than anything, because it told him that nobody was really listening; people were just there to be there. On top of this, the entire drill was getting old quickly. As Noel Redding once put it, "Four years on the road with the Experience is like ten years of life."

"In fact the band were never exactly over-rehearsed and it is obvious now that the electrifying 'newness' held it all together," Chris Welch later wrote in his biography of Hendrix. "As soon as the nightly routine began to pall, that's when the band began to fall apart. And the rest of Hendrix's years in England and in the States were spent searching for an alternative."

Hendrix chats with fans and photographers outside a Toronto, Canada, courthouse in May 1969. Canadian authorities had arrested him after finding illegal drugs in his carry-on luggage; after posting bail, Hendrix had performed his scheduled concert and then appeared in court to set a trial date.

Accompanied by a pair of supporters, Hendrix celebrates his acquittal on drug charges in December 1969.

He found one alternative in jamming. Hendrix spent more time in 1969 playing in low-key, informal settings that placed no restrictions on the set list, the song length, or the style of music played. Hendrix would walk into New York clubs like the Scene and Café Au Go Go with a guitar and spend a few hours with other players—some famous, some unknown. He could break for a beer without hassle or fuss from patrons, many of whom were, like the musicians, seeking refuge from the gawkers, groupies, and ever-increasing hype of the big-time rock scene. Hendrix could stretch out musically in these sessions, experiment, and play what he pleased. "I get more of a dreamier thing from the audience [in clubs]," Hendrix once said. "It's more of a thing that you go off into. . . . You don't forget about the audience, but you forget about all the paranoia."

Musicians and spectators lucky enough to be present say these impromptu jams yielded some of the most brilliant, beautiful playing they have ever heard. Hendrix, in turn, took great solace from these free-form late-night outings with strangers and friends. In the face of mounting business and personal pressures, retreating to the simplicity of his early playing days seemed to keep him stable and sane. It reminded him of why he had picked up a guitar in the first place.

At this point, rumors were flying that the Jimi Hendrix Experience was about to split. Everybody denied it. But the news of Noel Redding's new project, a band called Fat Mattress, only fed the speculation. And there was no denying that Hendrix and Redding, especially after the recording of *Electric Ladyland*, were practically at each other's throats. "Around 1969, we were so overwhelmed by money and the glamour of being so-called pop stars, we all forgot we were people," Redding later said.

Neither Hendrix nor Mike Jeffery was willing to lose Redding—not yet, anyway. So Fat Mattress got the opening slot on the Experience's next U.S. tour, which meant that Redding would be playing in two bands every night. By now Hendrix was fronting the highest-paid band in the world and leaving all the commercial details to Jeffery, a pure businessman with no background in music. Chas Chandler, who had married and settled down in London, retained a financial stake in the band and turned up at numerous shows. Hendrix asked him several times to return as manager. Chandler always said no.

The band's spring-summer U.S. tour, meanwhile, rolled through a series of ever-larger venues. The Experience was playing basketball and football stadiums now. Hendrix called the indoor shows

"Electric Church" and the outdoor shows "Sky Church." And the collection plate at these "churches" was fat enough to make a preacher blush: the Experience pulled down anywhere from $15,000 to $100,000 a performance, depending on ticket sales and the terms demanded by Jeffery, who was now in a position to ask for almost anything.

But money could not stop the crumbling of the band's morale; it could only convince everybody to stay together for another show, another payday. Money was cold comfort to Hendrix, who threw cash around like confetti and seemed to care very little about how it came or went. If anything, the money just reminded him of how trapped he now felt.

It also brought him unwanted friends. One evening before a concert in Newport, California, Hendrix was greeted in his dressing room by members of the Black Panther party, who mocked him for playing "white" music. The Panthers, a civil rights organization with the trappings of a paramilitary group, needed money to fund their activities, and they were trying to shame Hendrix into contributing. It is not clear whether they succeeded. But the Panthers were only one of many who made an issue of Hendrix's income.

That fall, following his appearance at Woodstock, Hendrix was literally kidnapped from a club by two hustlers who tried to obtain his contract from Jeffery as a ransom payment. Jeffery learned that the men were holding Hendrix at his own house in upstate New York. Jerry Morrison, an associate of Jeffery's, drove up to the house with a pair of enforcer types, overpowered the kidnappers, and rescued Hendrix, who was unharmed. In a television interview that summer with talk show host Dick Cavett, Hendrix had said, "The more money you make, the more you can sing the blues."

On May 3, before an Experience show at the Maple Leaf Gardens in Toronto, Canada, a policeman stopped Hendrix at Toronto's airport and searched his carry-on bag. The officer found three packets of heroin and a tube containing traces of hashish. Hendrix was arrested and charged with possession of drugs.

He posted $10,000 bail in time to play the Toronto show and turned in a loose, confident performance for a crowd that knew nothing about the bust. The story broke in the newspapers soon afterward. A judge ordered Hendrix to return to Toronto for preliminary hearings and a trial that could, if it ended with a conviction, send him to prison and derail his career. For all the disruption, the Experience/Fat Mattress caravan hardly missed a beat. Hendrix returned to Seattle in May for another show, and the tour rumbled onward through California and Hawaii.

The drug bust's effect on the Experience was mild compared to the friction between Hendrix and Redding, which finally reached the breaking point during the tour. On June 29, the Experience headlined the Denver Pop Festival at Mile High Stadium. To the complete surprise of everybody there—Redding included—Hendrix ended the show with this announcement: "This is the last gig we'll ever be playing together. "

Another 1960s supergroup had just bitten the dust. Redding flew to London and told interviewers he had resigned. Hendrix and Mitchell went to Hendrix's upstate New York house and started putting together a new band. Hendrix wanted a group that could reproduce onstage the rich, orchestral sound he was capable of creating in a studio. But he also wanted a connection to the music, and to the musicians, that he felt he had lost in the Experience. So he called some old friends: Billy Cox and Larry Lee, bandmates from his long-ago Nashville days. He also signed up two percussionists, Juma Sultan and Jerry Velez. The Experience was finished; Hendrix had a new band now and, he hoped, a new lease on his career. He introduced Billy Cox to the world on "The Tonight Show" in July and debuted the band, Gypsy Sons and Rainbows, in August at Woodstock.

Hendrix spoke fondly of the people at Woodstock who stayed three days to see him, but he had mixed feelings about the festival. Looking back three months later, he said, "Woodstock was groovy and all that, but anybody can get on a field and put a lot of kids in there and put band after band on. I don't particularly like the idea of groups after groups. It all starts merging together. They didn't give a damn about the sound equipment, the people way out there that couldn't hear nothing. So when you do festivals you're either going to have to have more days, or offer them more things besides music. You know, you should have little booths where they can buy this and that, where the Indians can come and sell their jewelry. A little circus here and there."

Hendrix also came away from Woodstock realizing that Gypsy Sons and Rainbows was not working. The band did some recording in New York in September and also played two more gigs, one at a summer street fair in Harlem, the other at a New York City club called Salvation. But in October, Hendrix summoned the five members to his hotel room and announced he was disbanding the group.

Mitch Mitchell returned to England. Hendrix, the only member of the original Experience left, asked Cox to stay on as bassist. They brought aboard an old acquaintance, Buddy Miles, on drums. Hendrix called this new trio Band of Gypsys. It was his third new lineup in the space of four months, but he was not done yet.

Hendrix spent much of November in the studio, amassing dozens of hours of taped recordings with Cox and Miles, on top of the material he had recorded with Gypsy Sons and Rainbows in September. As Harry Shapiro and Caesar Glebbeek have written, "By now both Warners and Track [Hendrix's British record label] were hopping up and down for some new material—Hendrix had been promising all kinds of projects to the press, but nothing had been delivered. Fragments of songs were liberally sprinkled through hundreds of hours of tape."

Hendrix was trying to use the studio time to simultaneously record and rehearse a new band. But distractions plagued him constantly. He was feuding with Jeffery and, uncharacteristically, beginning to worry that his manager might be stealing his money. He was also locked in a legal battle with Ed

A smiling Hendrix performs at the Fillmore East, January 12, 1970.

Chalpin, the New York producer who had signed Hendrix to a contract in his early days and now refused to accept a buyout or relinquish his rights to Hendrix's recordings. Track Records was refusing to pay Hendrix his British royalties until the lawsuits were settled.

Outside the studio, the whole world seemed to be going insane. Thousands of soldiers were returning home in coffins from Vietnam. College campuses were being rocked by student unrest. Hendrix attended a Rolling Stones concert in Altamont, California, that December and saw a young man stabbed to death in the crowd. The savagery of the act flew in the face of everything Hendrix felt about music and life.

Then there was the drug trial. Hendrix flew to Toronto and appeared in court on the morning of December 8, 1969, seven months after his arrest. The trial lasted three days, during which Hendrix, Chandler, and others testified that Hendrix had had no idea the drugs were inside his flight bag. The defense lawyer argued that some of Hendrix's fans, who were always lavishing gifts on him, must have discreetly tucked the drugs into his bag before the trip to Toronto. The jury listened to the testimony, deliberated for eight hours, and returned with a verdict—not guilty. Hendrix was cleared of all charges. He left the courtroom with a girlfriend, Jeanette Jacobs, and flashed a peace sign at the cameramen and reporters waiting outside. He was smiling.

Three weeks later, a familiar rhythmic noise drifted through the locked doors of Fillmore East into the wintry wind blowing down Manhattan's Second Avenue. Inside, sound poured from the amplifiers stacked like matching skylines on either side of Buddy Miles's drum kit. Hendrix, Cox, and Miles were jamming, rehearsing full-blast for the Band of Gypsys debut. The Fillmore was all but empty during these late December sessions; only the musicians, managers, and technical people moved between the floor and the stage. But on New Year's Eve, 1969, every seat in the place was filled. The host was Bill Graham, the savvy promoter who had booked Hendrix's early San Francisco shows at the original Fillmore. The Fillmore East performances— four in two days—would furnish the raw material for Hendrix' s first live album, *Band of Gypsys.*

Hendrix proved at the Fillmore East that he could still play brilliantly, no matter what crisis preceded him onstage or awaited him when he walked off. The live album, recorded to satisfy the conditions of his disputed contract with Ed Chalpin, was released on Capitol Records in April 1970. "If it had been up to me I would never have put it out," Hendrix once said. But *Band of Gypsys* contained several new songs and some breathtaking performances. Those two elements converged in "Machine Gun," an aggressive protest against violence in which Hendrix displayed his total mastery of technique and sound.

Unfortunately, the new band's debut was also its peak. The trio performed just once more, at the Winter Festival for Peace, an antiwar benefit concert held at New York's Madison Square Garden. That performance was disastrous; Hendrix, feeling sick and unable to play, walked offstage after two songs. End of show—end of Gypsys, too. Hendrix fired Buddy Miles, whose drumming did not fit his needs. Mike Jeffery was already on the phone to Mitch Mitchell and Noel Redding, telling them the Experience was being reborn. ♪

8

CASTLES MADE OF SAND

❧

IN THE EVER-SHIFTING circle of friends, groupies, and acolytes that surrounded Jimi Hendrix, nobody stood out like Devon Wilson. A tall, strikingly beautiful woman who was born in New York and had "come up hard," as the saying goes, Wilson found her way into the groupie circuit in the late 1960s. Once there, she moved with a queen's ease among rock's elite. She hung out with luminaries such as Mick Jagger and Eric Clapton when they came through New York, and she wore her reflected stature proudly. But she saved her greatest attention and affection for Hendrix, who came to trust her and made her part of his entourage.

It was not clear who had adopted whom. Wilson guarded Hendrix's turf fiercely. She stared down Jeffery when Hendrix would not. She was his confidant, lover, and mother figure. She also supplied him with drugs. She distrusted others in the circle, especially other women. But Devon knew Hendrix would never commit himself completely to her. He was as fickle about women as he was about musicians. He could not manage any one relationship for long; nor could he bring himself to completely sever his ties with anyone.

At Jeffery's urging, Mitchell and Redding flew to meet Hendrix in New York. The trio met with a *Rolling Stone* reporter to announce the Experience's return. But the "reunion" barely

In the spring of 1970, Hendrix went on tour again with a revamped band. His fans were as enthusiastic as ever, but he was plagued by the feeling that his music was growing stale.

outlasted the interview. Hendrix had already decided he could not play with Redding, who was told to go home. The bassist, hired and fired almost in one breath, returned to London. The revamped Experience lineup would now consist of Hendrix, Mitchell, and Billy Cox.

Hendrix's Cry of Love tour, launched in April 1970, coincided with the release of the *Band of Gypsys* album, which peaked at number five in the United States and number six in England. Fans were sticking with Hendrix despite all the recent chaos and turnover in his career and rewarding him with sold-out shows at arenas and festivals across the country. It was the first spring of a new decade, the 1970s; Hendrix felt he would have to outgrow the 1960s artistically or be stuck there forever while music moved on without him. "I've turned full circle," he told *Melody Maker* in 1970. "I'm right back where I started. I've given this era of music everything, but I still sound the same. My music's the same, and I can't think of anything to add to it in its present state."

Hendrix returned to Seattle in July for a concert at Sicks Stadium, where as a teenager he had seen Elvis Presley. Technical trouble made a wreck of the Gypsys show. But Hendrix spent the following day with his family and friends and it was, by all accounts, a pleasant visit. He left Seattle on July 27, 1970, for a scheduled show in Hawaii.

The Hawaii gig was not, strictly speaking, a concert. It was part of a strange and costly adventure launched by Hendrix's manager. Jeffery had secured money from Warner Bros. for a movie about the 1960s counterculture. The title was *Rainbow Bridge*. The story involved a crew of psychedelic explorers, young people who were into nature, spirituality, self-discovery, and mind-expanding drugs. The centerpiece of this pseudodocumentary was a Hendrix concert at the base of the legendary

Hendrix performs at the Isle of Wight Festival on August 30, 1970. He went on to tour a number of European cities, still struggling to find a groove with his bandmates.

Haleakala volcano on Maui—a plugged-in Sermon on the Mount.

The July 30 concert, called the Rainbow Bridge Vibratory Color/Sound Experiment, went fine. The film was another matter. In one of the kinder appraisals, rock critic Charles Shaar Murray dubbed it "the dumbest hippie movie ever made."

Hendrix played one more Hawaii date, in Honolulu, before returning to New York to attend the August 26 opening of his personal recording studio, Electric Lady, on West Eighth Street in

Greenwich Village. He and Eddie Kramer, the engineer, had already test-driven the $1 million state-of-the-art facility. Hendrix planned to spend a lot of time there once his schedule eased. He flew to London the day after the opening; the Experience had an August 30 date at the outdoor Isle of Wight Festival, Hendrix's first British gig in 18 months. "It has been a long time," he told a mass audience whose faces he could barely see in the gathering darkness. Despite the nostalgic mood, the concert did not go as well as it should have. Hendrix seemed distracted. Mitchell, who had not played with his old bandmate in almost a year, was stiff and under-rehearsed. The trio stumbled through its first few numbers, with Hendrix dropping lyrics, Mitchell missing beats, and Cox trying to hold everything

Monika Dannemann, Hendrix's companion, is consoled by a friend following Hendrix's sudden death in September 1970.

together with his bass. They finally locked on to each other, found a groove, and finished strong. But the first impression stuck with the critics, who painted Isle of Wight as a failure for Hendrix.

From England, Hendrix, Mitchell, and Cox retraced the original Experience's path across Sweden, Denmark, and Germany. Hendrix was exhausted from the travel and also ailing with a glandular condition that had flared up recently. He was becoming testy before shows. Twice in Denmark he had to be persuaded by friends to go onstage, and on one occasion he walked off after four songs, feeling he could play no more.

On September 6, 1970, the Experience headlined the outdoor Love and Peace Festival on the mist-shrouded Isle of Fehmarn, located in the Baltic Sea off the coast of Germany. The show was in trouble even before Hendrix arrived. Bikers had stormed the isle, robbed the box office, and taken over the parking concessions. Violence in the crowd delayed the band's appearance by a full day; Hendrix refused to play until calm prevailed. Organizers feared a riot. Hendrix, Cox, and Mitchell went on around noon on September 6 and played 13 songs. It was to be Hendrix's last official concert.

From Germany, Hendrix flew back to London, the city where everything had begun for him, and took a suite in the Cumberland Hotel near Marble Arch. He planned to rest and gather strength for whatever lay ahead. He had many decisions to make.

On September 11, Hendrix gave a charming, upbeat interview. "It's hard to decide what I'll do next," he said. "I'd like to have a small group and a large one, and maybe go touring with one of them." Asked about politics in music, he said, "Music is getting too heavy, almost to the state of unbearable. . . . When things get too heavy, just call me helium, the lightest gas known to man." He joked about getting away from it all by living in a tent, preferably one overlooking a mountain stream.

At the time, Hendrix was seeing a young woman named Monika Dannemann, a wealthy German heiress and figure-skating instructor he had met in Düsseldorf in 1968. The two had stayed in touch ever since, and now in London they were together every day. Hendrix's room at the Cumberland was usually empty while he stayed at the Samarkand Hotel, in Dannemann's apartment.

On Tuesday, September 15, Hendrix and Dannemann went to Ronnie Scott's, a London nightclub, to see Eric Burdon and his new band, War, on the first of two nights. On Wednesday, Hendrix called Chas Chandler. "He asked me to produce for him again," Chandler recalled. "He rang me again on the Thursday and we got to discussing the design for a cover. He said he was going to America to pick up some tapes for his next album. He was happy, but he had been recording for over a year and a half and hadn't really produced anything."

Hendrix went to see Sly and the Family Stone, the reigning funk band of the day, on Wednesday night at the Lyceum, and after that show he jammed with Eric Burdon and War at Ronnie Scott's. Burdon remembers Hendrix as moody but motivated enough to play.

Thursday was the sort of day off that busy rock stars say they rarely have—nothing was scheduled and nothing required. Hendrix and Dannemann went shopping. They ran into some friends and made plans to attend a dinner party that night. Hendrix swung by his room at the Cumberland and made several phone calls, one of them to his New York lawyer, Henry Steingarten, with whom he discussed future alternatives: Hendrix had only a month left on his contract with Mike Jeffery. Later,

he took a call at the hotel from Mitchell, who said he and Ginger Baker, the former drummer for Cream, were going to meet Sly Stone.

"Is there any chance of a play?" Hendrix asked, clearly excited.

"Funny you should say that, yeah," Mitchell replied. "The idea is we're all going down to the Speakeasy for a jam."

Hendrix said he would be there around midnight and hung up. Mitchell waited at the

Friends and relatives carry Hendrix's coffin out of Seattle's Dunlap Baptist Church on October 1, 1970. The funeral service was attended by numerous luminaries from the music world and was covered by more than 200 reporters and photographers.

Speakeasy until closing time, 4:00 A.M. Hendrix never came.

At 3:00, Hendrix and Dannemann returned to her apartment, after going to the dinner party and having a nightcap. Before going to bed, Hendrix took some sleeping tablets. He fell into a deep, drugged sleep.

Dannemann woke the next morning, Friday, and found Hendrix still asleep. She went out to buy cigarettes. She returned and padded quietly about the apartment, taking care not to disturb Hendrix, although she knew he had an appointment with his record company that afternoon. Finally, she thought about waking him. She sat down near the edge of the bed and studied his face—and saw that something was wrong. A trickle of darkish liquid was running from Hendrix's mouth. She bolted out of her chair. "I tried immediately to wake him up and I just couldn't wake him up," Dannemann later said. "And I tried all different ways, shaking and everything and I just couldn't."

At 11:18, Dannemann phoned for an ambulance, which arrived nine minutes later. White-coated paramedics rushed into the apartment. They checked Hendrix's vital signs; he was still alive. They rolled him onto a stretcher. The ambulance left the hotel at 11:45. Inside the vehicle, the paramedics lifted Hendrix from the stretcher and placed him upright in a chair, holding his head back. His eyes were still closed.

The ambulance reached St. Mary Abbotts Hospital shortly after noon. Hendrix was still alive when he reached the hospital, but he soon went into cardiac arrest. Although doctors scrambled to revive him, the line on the heart monitor remained flat. A doctor pronounced Hendrix dead at 12:45 P.M. He was 27.

An autopsy revealed that Hendrix had reacted to the combination of barbiturates—his sleeping pills—and the alcohol he had consumed earlier that night. The mixture had upset Hendrix's stomach and had caused him to vomit, but it also caused his throat to close up; this reaction restricted his breathing and prevented him from clearing his stomach. The vomit had trickled down his windpipe, collapsing a lung and causing him to suffocate. The coroner delivered an "open verdict," meaning there was not enough information to rule Hendrix's death either a suicide or an accident. Most of those who have studied the facts, as well as those who knew Hendrix best, remain convinced that his death was purely accidental.

After the coroner's inquest, Hendrix's body was flown home to Seattle for an October 1 funeral at Dunlap Baptist Church. The pallbearers were all friends and relatives of Hendrix's, including his former bandmate James Thomas. Grandmother Nora, now 86 years old, came to say good-bye with Hendrix's father, his brother, and his stepsister. Mitch Mitchell, Noel Redding, Buddy Miles, and Devon Wilson were among the mourners. Despite his previous differences with Hendrix, Redding wept during the service, and Miles was so grief-stricken that he could barely stand. Jazz legend Miles Davis and blues guitarist Johnny Winter also came to pay their respects. Some 200 reporters and photographers stood behind a cordon outside the church, along with a host of Hendrix fans. Hendrix was buried at Greenwood Cemetery in a simple grave beneath a plaque inscribed with the name his father had given him: JAMES MARSHALL HENDRIX, 1942–1970. ◑

9

CRY OF LOVE

❦

THE DAY BEFORE he died, Hendrix wrote a song called "The Story of Life (Slow)." The handwritten lyrics turned up among his belongings in Monika Dannemann's apartment. The music remained in his head and will never be known. The lyric read in part: "The story / of life is quicker / than the wink of an eye / The story of love / is hello and goodbye / Until we meet again."

The Cry of Love, Hendrix's last studio album, was released in America on March 6, 1971, six months after his death. The 10-song album, which continued Hendrix's explorations outside the confines of hard rock, reached number two in England and number three on the U.S. charts. It spent 39 weeks on the American charts, a run that most living artists would envy.

Hendrix died without making a will, leading to a number of court battles that were finally resolved in 1995, when his family secured the rights to all the material he had left behind. The family's struggle to safeguard Hendrix's legacy was spurred by the remarkable freshness of his appeal. Hendrix made music that has flourished in his absence and has found an audience among people who were born after he died. His albums still sell 3 million to 4 million copies a year.

At the same time, few artists are as closely identified with the spirit of the 1960s as is Hendrix. "Purple Haze," "Voodoo Chile," and his aston-

This striking tribute to Hendrix was painted in 1993 by Dan Hitchcock. The mural adorns a downtown Seattle building that once housed Myers Music Store, where Al Hendrix bought Jimi his first electric guitar in 1959.

ishing version of "The Star-Spangled Banner" reappear in American culture like the sirens of a lost age. Hendrix wrote the sound track for a decade, but despite his fears of being passed by, his music has lasted into the generations that followed. The image of Hendrix wringing notes from his trademark Stratocaster has become as familiar in some circles as George Washington's face on a dollar bill, and the story of the youngster who hears Hendrix for the first time and sprints to the nearest guitar shop is part of American lore.

Hendrix's influence resounds in the playing of every guitarist schooled on his licks, and his leading disciples have included Stevie Ray Vaughan, Prince, Vernon Reid, Eric Johnson, Joe Satriani, Mike Stern, Pat Metheny, John Scofield, Steve Vai, and Mike McCreedy. Each of these musicians has paid tribute to Hendrix either by covering his songs or quoting his style. "I've been imitated so well, I've heard people copy my mistakes," Hendrix once said.

But Hendrix's influence reaches far beyond the fretboard. Despite his lack of formal schooling in music, Hendrix's sense of melody, composition, and song structure have filtered into the highly complex and formalized world of jazz. Hendrix blew down the fire walls between jazz, rock, blues, and rhythm and blues. Even at the height of his rock career, he was winning the admiration of talented jazz artists who saw him moving very deliberately in their direction. "Hendrix would have been one of the jazz greats," the legendary trumpeter Miles Davis once declared.

Some observers feel Hendrix has yet to receive his due as a songwriter, but the acknowledgment of his gifts in this area is growing. A popular classical string ensemble, the Kronos Quartet, pays homage to Hendrix with a chamber-music version of "Purple Haze." The Hendrix tribute album *Stone*

Free, released in 1993, includes 14 songs by rock, rap, blues, jazz, and classical artists who reinterpret and elaborate on Hendrix's musical ideas while staying true to their spirit.

Hendrix created a "Seattle sound" long before the rise of "grunge" bands such as Nirvana, Pearl Jam, and Soundgarden. His presence, especially in the music of the latter two bands, is as unmistakable as his general influence on dress and stage theatrics, which is vividly demonstrated in Prince's 1984 film, *Purple Rain.*

In the years since his death, Hendrix's music has influenced countless young musicians, including the artist formerly known as Prince, pictured here in a scene from his film Purple Rain.

Flanked by Neil Young (right) and Noel Redding, Al Hendrix is overcome by emotion as his son Jimi is inducted into the Rock and Roll Hall of Fame in January 1992.

Those who have criticized Hendrix's politics—or lack of politics—and his naïveté about the world have overlooked the motivating power of his music. Grounded in blues, the idiom of the poor, it was a voice of release, a "cry of love" that, like all great blues, transcended the pain and the physical hardships that gave the music its soul. Hendrix transmitted what he heard inside him back to the limitless universe he seemed to capture and channel through his playing. For some listeners, this was nothing less than revolutionary.

To people around him, Hendrix could seem like somebody just along for the ride, a tourist on his own bus, going wherever the road led, leaving details to others. It was a posture that seemed to fit his gentle, undemanding nature and his live-and-

let-live view of things. But there was no such pas-
sivity inside, where Hendrix set his brain and heart
loose to work feverishly over his musical ideas; nor
on a stage, where this rangy, tangle-haired man
could rivet several thousand people with the sight
and sound of his body and guitar merging into one
dynamic force.

Increasingly, Hendrix was trying to convey love,
peace, harmony, and tolerance through his playing. These were the ideals he clung to in confus-
ing, hostile times, and music was a way to share
those gifts. "I can't express myself easy in conver-
sation—the words just don't come out right," he
once said. "But when I get up on stage—well, that's
my whole life. That's my religion. My music is electric church music, if by 'church' you mean 'religion.' I am electric religion."

For all the records, films, and books about
Hendrix, he remains a mystery. Gaps exist in the
chronology of his life, particularly in his youth,
when his travels took him out of circulation, beyond
the reach of biographers and archivists. Questions
linger about the circumstances surrounding his
death. And the sources of his musical inspiration
may never be fully explained. How did one man
produce so much music in just a few years? Even his
best friends say they never got close enough to
know. "Well I don't really know if I have friends
or not," Hendrix once said. Hendrix existed in his
own sphere; the rest of the world only got glimpses
of him, mostly through music.

"My music is my personal diary," he once said,
"a release of all my inner feelings, aggression, ten-
derness, sympathy—everything." It is a diary whose
pages music fans keep turning. For Hendrix, the
story of life continues. &

APPENDIX:
SELECTED DISCOGRAPHY

———— ❧ ————

1967	*Are You Experienced?*
	Axis: Bold as Love
1968	*Electric Ladyland*
1969	*Smash Hits*
1970	*Band of Gypsys*
1971	*Historic Performances Recorded at the Monterey International Pop Festival*
	The Cry of Love
	Rainbow Bridge
	Isle of Wight
1972	*Hendrix in the West*
	War Heroes
1973	*Soundtrack from the film* Jimi Hendrix
1975	*Crash Landing*
	Midnight Lightnin'
1978	*The Essential Jimi Hendrix*
1979	*The Essential Jimi Hendrix, Vol. 2*
1980	*Nine to the Universe*
1982	*The Jimi Hendrix Concerts*
1988	*Radio One*
1995	*Voodoo Soup*

CHRONOLOGY

1942   Born Johnny Allen Hendrix on November 27, in Seattle, Washington

1946   Renamed James Marshall Hendrix by his father

1951   Al and Lucille Hendrix divorce; Jimmy and his brother begin living with their father

1959   Receives his first electric guitar as a gift from his father; enrolls in Seattle's Garfield High School; joins local band, the Rocking Kings

1960   Drops out of high school; continues to play with the Rocking Kings and the Tomcats

1961   Enlists in the U.S. Army and is assigned to the 101st Airborne Division

1962   With Billy Cox, forms the King Kasuals at Fort Campbell, Kentucky, and plays on local army bases; discharged from the army after injuring his back in a parachute jump

1963   Begins career as a professional guitarist, playing behind established artists such as Jackie Wilson, Sam Cooke, Hank Ballard, Little Richard, and the Supremes

1964   Arrives in New York City and wins first prize in the Amateur Night Contest at the Apollo Theatre in Harlem; begins to tour with the Isley Brothers

1965   Tours with Little Richard for several months; joins Curtis Knight and the Squires

1966   Forms his own band, Jimmy James and the Blue Flames; meets Chas Chandler and agrees to let Chandler be his manager; travels to London and forms the Jimi Hendrix Experience; band debuts in France in October and releases its first single, "Hey Joe," in December

1967	Hendrix releases his first album, *Are You Experienced?*; makes U.S. debut at the Monterey Pop Festival; releases second album, *Axis: Bold as Love*
1968	Jimi Hendrix Experience launches its first U.S. tour as headline act and records its third studio album, *Electric Ladyland*
1969	Noel Redding quits the band; Hendrix plays at Woodstock
1970	Hendrix embarks on his last U.S. tour; releases *Band of Gypsys* album; dies on September 18 in London, England

FURTHER READING

Henderson, David. *Scuse Me While I Kiss the Sky: The Life of Jimi Hendrix.* New York: Bantam, 1981.

Hopkins, Jerry. *Hit & Run: The Jimi Hendrix Story.* New York: Perigee, 1983.

Knight, Curtis. *Jimi: An Intimate Biography of Jimi Hendrix.* New York: Star, 1974.

MacDermott, John. *Jimi Hendrix Sessions: The Complete Studio Recording Sessions, 1963–1970.* Boston: Little, Brown, 1995.

Mitchell, Mitch, and John Platt. *Jimi Hendrix: Inside the Experience.* New York: St. Martin's, 1990.

Murray, Charles Shaar. *Crosstown Traffic: Jimi Hendrix and the Rock 'n' Roll Revolution.* New York: St. Martin's, 1989.

Sampson, Victor. *Hendrix: An Illustrated Biography.* London: Proteus, 1984.

Shapiro, Harry, and Caesar Glebbeek. *Jimi Hendrix: Electric Gypsy.* New York: St. Martin's, 1992.

Welch, Chris. *Hendrix: A Biography.* New York: Flash, 1973.

INDEX

PICTURE CREDITS

SEAN PICCOLI covers politics, culture, and entertainment for the *Washington Times* in Washington, D.C. He received a B.A. in journalism from the University of Wisconsin in Madison, and he plays guitar on weekends.

NATHAN IRVIN HUGGINS, one of America's leading scholars in the field of black studies, helped select the titles for the BLACK AMERICANS OF ACHIEVEMENT series, for which he also served as senior consulting editor. He was the W.E.B. Du Bois Professor of History and Afro-American Studies at Harvard University and the director of the W.E.B. Du Bois Institute for Afro-American Research at Harvard. He received his doctorate from Harvard in 1962 and returned there as a professor in 1980 after teaching at Columbia University, the University of Massachusetts, Lake Forest College, and the California State University, Long Beach. He was the author of four books and dozens of articles, including *Black Odyssey: The Afro-American Ordeal in Slavery, The Harlem Renaissance,* and *Slave and Citizen: The Life of Frederick Douglass,* and was associated with the Children's Television Workshop, National Public Radio, the Boston Athenaeum, the Museum of Afro-American History, the Howard Thurman Educational Trust, and Upward Bound. Professor Huggins died in 1989, at the age of 62, in Cambridge, Massachusetts.